When the Master Relents

The Neglected Short
Fictions of Henry James

Studies in Modern Literature, No. 80

A. Walton Litz, General Series Editor

Professor of English
Princeton University

Consulting Editor:
Daniel Mark Fogel
Professor of English
Louisiana State University
Editor, *Henry James Review*

Other Titles in This Series

When the Master Relents
The Neglected Short Fictions of Henry James

by
George Bishop

U·M·I Research Press

Ann Arbor / London

Produced and distributed by
UMI Research Press
an imprint of
University Microfilms Inc.
Ann Arbor, Michigan 48106

Library of Congress Cataloging in Publication Data

Bishop, George, 1955-
When the master relents.

(Studies in modern literature ; no. 80)
Bibliography: p.
Includes index.
1. James, Henry, 1843-1916—Criticism and
interpretation.   I. Title.   II. Series.
PS2124.B52   1988   813'.4   87-25543
ISBN 0-8357-1826-3 (alk. paper)

British Library CIP data is available.

For Anne

I am conscious of much to say of these numerous small productions as a family—a family indeed quite organised as such, with its proper representatives, its "heads," its subdivisions and its branches, its poor relations perhaps not least: its unmistakeable train of poor relations in fact, the very poorer, the poorest of whom I am, in family parlance, for this formal appearance in society, "cutting" without a scruple. These repudiated members, some of them, for that matter, well-nourished and substantial presences enough, with their compromising rustiness plausibly, almost touchingly dissimulated, I fondly figure as standing wistful but excluded, after the fashion of the outer fringe of the connected whom there are not carriages enough to convey from the church—whether (for we have our choice of similes) to the wedding-feast or to the interment!

Henry James, Preface to *The Aspern Papers*

The Master

Henry James

Contents

Acknowledgments

Early drafts of the manuscript have benefitted from the comments and suggestions of several colleagues, especially Henry Sussman, William Beatty Warner, John Carlos Rowe and Daniel Mark Fogel. My thinking about this project, and my desire to complete it, were sharpened by a number of friends at SUNY Buffalo, notably John Lick, Kathy Boone and Carole Southwood. Thanks also to my colleagues at D'Youville College for their support and interest. Melanie Wisner of the Houghton Library at Harvard kindly provided her expert assistance in obtaining photographs and checking journals.

Versions of chapter 2, on "A Bundle of Letters," and chapter 3, on "Glasses," originally appeared in *The Henry James Review* and *Criticism*, respectively. I am grateful to the publishers of those journals for permission to reprint that material. The photographs of Henry James found here are reproduced by permission of the Houghton Library and Mr. Alexander James.

Special thanks are due Neil Schmitz, teacher and friend, for introducing me to James, and for being over many years my most discerning reader, and a constant source of encouragement.

My greatest debt is to my wife, Anne, for understanding.

1

Discharging the Jamesian Canon:
An Introduction

There is an element of farce in any introduction. Written, as is so often the case, the very last of all, an introduction demands an exhibition of mastery of the subsequent material sufficient to produce a summarization, and to sketch the broad outlines of the text just beginning to unfold. But the rhetorical constraints inherent in such an undertaking demand as well in many instances the supposed deferral of masterful completeness, in order to provide the reader with a sense of gentle entrance. Such considerations, problematic in themselves, are magnified here by the fact that it is these very issues which are at stake throughout my enterprise. The notion of "mastery," and the fictional mechanisms of its withholding . . . but I am already ahead of myself. Let us begin at the beginning, by drawing some conclusions.

This study takes as its object a handful of short fictions by Henry James. Written at various points in his career, these fictions are united here not by a proposed commonality of thematic or formal characteristics, but by the simple fact that they have been consistently and thoroughly ignored. When they are read at all—a rare occurrence—they tend to be either systematically misread or quickly judged to be in some way inferior. The result in either case is the same—the firm exclusion of these texts from the established Jamesian canon. One need hardly mention the profound effect of such an exclusion on what is chosen to be anthologized, taught, or addressed in critical forums. While the reviewer is limited to a crude frontal assault in dealing with an author's rejecta, the academic critic wields the far more devastating weapon of silence.

The issue of canon-formation and persistence has been much considered lately, and from various points of view. One of the most perceptive readings of this controversy has been presented by Frank Kermode, who makes bold to offer a guideline for further discussion when he states that, "in short, the only rule common to all interpretation games, the sole family resemblance between them, is that the canonical work, so endlessly discussed, must be assumed to have permanent value and, which is really the same thing, perpetual modernity."[1] There is

sufficient lightness in the paradox of the term "perpetual modernity" to make room
for its use, did it not mask a serious problem, and act as yet another diversion.
"Modernity" in Kermode's sense is seen as a feature belonging to the work. It
inhabits the text, as a quality with a discernible location that is [found by a critical
act, which is separated from the work itself.] The bracket is crucial here, for it
marks the place where we are willing to ignore, by the metaphysics of definition,
the issue we have staked out for ourselves. (As Kermode says, the work "must be
assumed to have" these qualities.) Thus, the matter of determining canonicity
cannot be separated from the instances of its determining—it is only as reified
discourse that it exists separately, as object. As discourse, its production is, as
Michel Foucault has noted, "controlled, selected, organised and redistributed
according to a certain number of procedures, whose role is to avert its powers and
its dangers, to cope with chance events, to evade its ponderous, awesome
materiality."[2]

The importation of Foucault here highlights another closely related issue.
There is a point at which any discussion of the canon becomes necessarily
theoretized (though not necessarily theoretical), occurring at the moment when we
are threatened with emergence into the practical. That is to say, it is safer, by far,
to note the theoretical implications of problems of defining the canon, the question
of its maintenance and the question of agency with regard to that maintenance,
when those questions are divorced from the actuality of individual readers reading
and writers writing. On the one hand, the relations of power and influence
manifested there are such that their naked emergence is at least a matter of bad
taste. And, at the same time, if the question of canonicity is one of discourse, or of
paradigm, then the question of individual human contact must by definition drop
out, despite the irony of being engaged in a "humanistic" enterprise. When one is
approached, as professors often are, with the question of "who" decides what is
"great literature," a bemused and tight-lipped smile may after all be the right
answer, if to the wrong question. For there may, in fact, be compelling reasons
why the operative power of the canon should be withstood, and not rigorously
investigated as such, in that the relations involved there do in some very real sense
determine the state of our collective enterprise, and account for its valuation, or at
least the criteria of its valuation. On the other hand, if the ingenuousness of the
student's question is entered, we find the equally real acknowledgment that there
is "no one" who makes these determinations—and to blame it on the wisdom of the
ages, on a series of distinguished predecessors, is to euphemize the case
conveniently. Thus, in an appeal to the transcendence of humanistic value, we
ignore the instances of those values being circumvented by a discourse that may or
may not subscribe to them, and moreover, we ignore the much more important
issue of whether humanistic values operate within "discourse" at all.[3]

The flight into the theoretical and the generalized, then, can serve as a
mechanism to avoid the realities of canonical practice. The frustration of not

having the power to affect the canon, and the frustration of being unable to locate those who do—this becomes of import only when the conclusions rendered affect, or perhaps even victimize, individuals, in definite and accountable ways, at certain times and places. Conversely, participation in canonical discourse can serve as a route to avoid such disenfranchisement. In any event, this issue attracts our attention, in its status as simulacrum of the larger issue of value in the twentieth century. If disenchantment with the old explanations and accounts of value is a distinguishing feature of modernism, perhaps the task of post-modernism, or its definition, lies in the attention to the residuum, itself vast, that lies around the ruins of old questions.

But that does not prevent those old questions from being pursued, on a large scale, and in a manner that ascends to the comic as it nears a crucial point. If the canon is to be recognized in its operations, we need to acknowledge its function as prescriptive, and not merely descriptive. Recent and cogent challenges to the canon, especially those raised from the locus of special interest—such as those by theoreticians accepting the labels of feminist or Marxist, for example—have illustrated exactly this. But there we often find the tendency to offer, if not demand, an "alternative" canon—the issue then is not "opening up" the canon, or destroying it, but *replacing* it. Curiously, such efforts, while providing the smug pleasure of a cautious radicalism, are thoroughly acceptable institutionally, and become quickly reabsorbed into traditional discursive practice—for what is hidden in the anticanonical onslaught is the desire to belong to the mainstream. Though one may deplore a loss of homeland, the appropriation of that space at the cost of current occupants only perpetuates the rituals of displacement and exclusion that are at the center of the establishment of discursive parameters. The issue then is not the canon itself, despite the rush of words to that effect, if the end of the discussion is merely to reassert the power of the canon under a different flag.

We know as well that canons can shift, that their contours can change over time. Such changes are retrospectively apparent, yet usually ascribed to the agencies of discovery and correction. But as long as we debate the limits of the canon, we keep it in place, because such a debate deflects us from the source of the canon, which is the will to knowledge and the will to power. The erection and maintenance of the canon is achieved by the perpetuation of a discourse that already contains the assumptions we tell ourselves are demonstrated independently by that canon. Thus, the act of challenging not "the" canon, but "a" canon (or better yet, for our purposes here, "the Master") contains an element of radicalism that threatens to expose not the thing but its constitutive process, and if that happens, there is no reason for commentary to continue. For a collective venture which already perceives its foundation as somewhat tenuous, such a possibility seems inherently desperate.

The process of canon formation in the case of a single author has ostensibly involved the selection of certain works from the corpus of that author upon which is conferred the status of "value" and "permanence." Such a selection proceeds on the basis of an independently established criterion of judgment, itself usually an extrapolation from the works in question. It is my contention that the criterion tacitly employed in the production and maintenance of the Jamesian canon is intimately related to and dependent upon the notion of Henry James as the Master. That the figure of James the Master is familiar to students of American literature comes as a welcome relief, since even as it is subjected to scrutiny it tends to slip inexorably away from definition, and into caricature—a point readily apparent in the arena of biography. Though the excesses of Theodora Bosanquet and Ford Madox Ford are execrated, it is precisely the distillation of those excesses that serve as the most pungent features of the Master's persona—and all this despite the historically certain image of a rotund Henry James in gaily striped waistcoat clumsily pedaling a bicycle through the Sussex countryside. Only through a mastery sufficiently potent to resolve apparent contradictions into an umbrella of biographical consistency is it possible to countenance a full five volumes of biography devoted to a man to whom next to nothing ever happened.

With respect to James's fictional productions, the image of the Master comes only a bit more clearly into focus. It implies above all the notion of technical perfection, and an excellence of execution capable of answering in full any charge of inconsistency—witness the fact that the renowned Jamesian "ambiguity" is rarely if ever raised as an objection, but is instead touted as proof of the author's sterling craftsmanship. Moreover, the fullness of the Master's control over his artistic forms and methods extends even to the point where it sets the standards for judgment against which other efforts are measured: the Master, occupying the seat of authority, both ratifies and coopts the determination of canonicity. This peculiar reversal accounts in large part for the reverence Jamesian critics demonstrate for the Master's critical pronouncements—widely scattered throughout the essays and prefaces—despite their manifest rhetorical convolution, their mutual incompatibility, and the fact that they are rarely applicable in critical practice.

Despite this tendency to authorial lionization, however, we recognize that "the Master" is itself a fiction, created by James and applied by his critics, and perpetuated by both text and reading, for the sake of consistency and identity, in order to ground the critical discourse in an illusion of historicity and make possible the repetition that constitutes a critical discourse. The Master is the one who, in Foucault's terms, "implants, into the troublesome language of fiction, its unities, its coherence, its links with reality."[4] What we tend to miss is this: James also textualizes the functions of the Master. The Master is inscribed repeatedly in his texts, and marks the spot where that inscription itself allows commentary to proceed, to be repeated. Ordinarily, we recognize this only insofar as the emergence of the Master guarantees the conditions of his emergence—where he operates *as* Master, in permitting and authorizing the repetition of criticism.

By way of illustration, I take here the case of an acknowledged Jamesian "master-work." "The Figure in the Carpet" remains a text to be beaten—it challenges the reader, the critic, to account for it. It has received endless attention lately, as having metonymic value as the descriptor of theoretical disputes, and as acting as a mirror for the desires of its readers. In a sense, it would seem to have the quality of "perpetual modernity" that would define the canonical text, by virtue of its ability to somehow produce, account for or sustain a rush of critical activity of a type impossible only a few years ago. One of the most comprehensive and perceptive of recent readings of "The Figure in the Carpet," and of the critical controversy surrounding it, is that of Ross Chambers in *Story and Situation.*[5] Chambers offers the contention that, in the contest of decipherment between George Corvick and the unnamed narrator of this story for the "secret" of Hugh Vereker's work, "Gwendolen is the *reward* of an already successful critical performance, not a means of achieving such success."[6] Though I applaud Chambers's attention to the often neglected character Gwendolen Erme, it seems to me that his conclusion here is misleading. The narrator specifically informs us that Corvick understands Vereker's secret only *after* his marriage to Erme is contemplated, if not certain, and that the revelation seems to him to be somehow the result of a mysterious and unspecified joint venture. I would contend therefore that the understanding of Vereker's secret comes only after a committed withdrawal from the pursuit of it that marks the narrator. Corvick's trip to India before his marriage signals a shift in consciousness away from the egocentric quest for distinction that characterizes the narrator, and the Western culture he inhabits, and Erme's authorship of a novel entitled *Overmastered* may well refer not to excessive subjugation, but to a "mastery" that is "over."

Most tellingly, the issue of Gwendolen Erme leads us to a consideration of the characters' names. One need not look as far as the Celtic origins of "Erme" here, when James's Notebooks contain repeated examples of his recording lists of possible character names, one often distinguished from the next only by phonetic rearrangement. An entry of October 5, 1899—only one of several such lists—contains among others the following plays on sound: "Berther—Champer—Server," "Dandridge—Wantridge—Wantrage," "Charlick—Carrick—Dearth—Mellet—Pellet—Brine—Bromage," while an entry of March 4, 1895, contains the revealing "Rimmington—Roof—Carvick—Corvick—Burbeck."[7] The phonetic similarity between "Vereker" and "Corvick" is apparent, with the latter containing all the consonants of the former, without the corresponding vowels. It is "Erme" that will supply that lack, so that the junction of Corvick-Erme can perform as a kind of sloppy anagram—Verickor-Vereker—with the remainder that is cast aside being the redoubtable "me," the signal of the unnamed narrator's cleverness and egotistic obsession. The capture of Vereker's "secret," then, lies not in Vereker's text, but out of it, in a kind of cancellation through approximation. The marriage of Corvick and Erme makes possible the meshing that will write "the name of the author," and therefore end the quest; and their possession of the secret is always, like Vereker's, completely apparent, in the public sign of their joint identity.

I have offered this reading, however fragmentary, of a portion of "The Figure in the Carpet" as a contrast to that of Professor Chambers; and not as a corrective, but as an instance of how this text can sustain a pluralism of competing readings. As Chambers says elsewhere, "Vereker's true superiority over the critic does not lie in his possession of a secret so much as it results from his successful deployment of discursive strategies for which the younger man is not a match. . . . In this light, the text-critic relationship appears as one between a rhetorically masterful text and a reader ill equipped to 'lay it bare.' "[8] This inadequacy becomes, for Chambers, a "motivating factor" in the story; for me, that motivation extends outside the story, into the critical world. That is to say, the critical act, as the perpetuation of interpretation, has its own value previous to the text it operates upon. The relationship of power that circumscribes the narrator and Vereker is already existent for us, and prior to our encounter with this text, or with any text.

One of the figures in "The Figure in the Carpet" thus lies in the multiplicity of readings that it authorizes and provides a site for. It hardly matters what the content of those readings are—whether they agree or disagree on the nature or even the presence of the secret, whether they focus on the text as "undecidable" or not—the point is that something here allows for the recurrent commentary, the challenges of subsequent discourses.[9] As Chambers notes, "the *je ne sais quoi* of literature is the *sine qua non* of criticism: unless the text is conceived as having some undefined quality that needs defining, an inexplicit something that should be made explicit, there is no role for interpretation."[10] The assumption of that "something" or other, made by Corvick and seconded by the narrator, is shared by us, as critical readers—our right and our need to exist is grounded therein. One of the most problematic features of "The Figure in the Carpet" is that this text also contains a parody of the critical act—and much has recently been written on the circumstances determining that act—but all that is written assumes and depends upon the opening to speak critically, to respond. If the quest in "The Figure in the Carpet" is ironic or humorous, if the searcher is monster or hero, responsible agent or victim, it simply doesn't matter—since the relationship of critic to text there authorizes us to do the same kinds of operations that the narrator does, with a subsequent and sometimes explicit feeling of superiority, while making the same mistakes. Whether the role of the critical respondent is ironic, comical, sad or melodramatic, it is always nonetheless engaged *as* critic, and in arguing endlessly about the qualities of that criticism, we deflect our attention from the question of the question itself—what accounts for the critic's place?

"In short, the rivalry, the struggle for power among James's characters is still pursued in the discourse of their descendants . . . the critical history of the work reproduces what, precisely, is at issue in the work."[11] Ross Chambers's comment on this question is particularly direct, but stops just a bit short, in leaving the impression that that struggle for power is to be regarded as a static entity, capable of location and description. I would contend that it is best seen as a motivating force, accounting for the elevation of "The Figure in the Carpet" to the status of master-work, simply because it can act as a stage for these struggles of "mastery" to be carried out. This is alone enough to justify and account for all the questions of the Master's relations to text and critic, whether that Master be Hugh Vereker or Henry James. The final definition of the Master himself is unnecessary (and perhaps even undesirable), as long as we are assured that the act of defining can always go on, in perpetuity. Thus, the critical history of the work does not only *re*-produce what is at issue in the work, it *produces* that issue.

If "The Figure in the Carpet" occupies its place within the Jamesian canon by virtue of its rendition of a peculiarly desirable form of interpretative mastery, what then do we make of those texts of Henry James wherein the notion of mastery, in whatever form, is ironized, humorized, demystified or denied? Texts that would seemingly refuse to allow the room for critical maneuverings of any kind? Evidently, these texts cannot exist: since they refuse the conditions of their place among the Master's works, they comprise by definition that residuum that lies outside the canon.

The elucidation of James's noncanonical works thus takes on an added dimension, best seen as a point of contrast. Taking, in a deliberately oversimplified example, the fiction of Kafka: if we were to contend that Kafka's canon is constituted on the basis of his exposition of "alienation," then the inclusion of "The Metamorphosis" and *The Castle* is obvious, and the concomitant exclusion of, let's say, "The Bucket Rider," would hardly be surprising. Further, if one were to contest the exclusion of the latter, a simple procedure of resolution would emerge: the criterion for the determination of canonical status is specified (here, some sort of demarcation of the perimeters of "alienation"), "The Bucket Rider" is examined for points of correspondence, and a decision is reached. Even the irony of Kafka's authorship of *The Trial* is insufficient to avoid this inexorable verdict. Similar discriminations, based on different criteria, could be drawn between *The Sound and the Fury* and *Soldier's Pay*, between *Moby-Dick* and *Mardi*. The case of James, on the other hand, is not quite so easily handled. If, as I have suggested, the determination of the Jamesian canon rests upon an appeal to the notion of the Master, then it must be remembered that that same notion of the Master grants the authorization for judgment which in turn circumscribes the entire question of canonicity. To raise the issue of the Master's noncanonical works is therefore not merely to question the construction of ideological boundaries in the critical fiction of a particular authorial voice: these works harbor the possibility of an implicit critique of, if not an outright challenge to, the idea of the canon itself.

We come here, parenthetically, to the notion of a "minor literature," as defined by Deleuze and Guattari, and refined by Louis Renza.[12] Their postulation of a minor literature would apparently demand the replacement of our obsession with the individual author with that of a collective perspective on authorship: "Indeed, precisely because talent isn't abundant in a minor literature, there are no possibilities for an individuated enunciation that would belong to this or that 'master' and that could be separated from a collective enunciation. Indeed, scarcity of talent is in fact beneficial and allows the conception of something other than a literature of masters; what each author says individually already constitutes a common action."[13] This seems problematic, however, in that as soon as we posit a place and person, we posit an entire discourse of authorship, even to the extent of a literature desiring that it be "authored"—that is, the work's seeming facility to construct and present the voice that we find there, whether the desire for that presentation resides in the work, the "author," or the discourse that binds both. Renza notes that what minor literature needs is a "minor criticism," while he remains aware of the fact that any criticism institutionalizes its own action, and drags in the notion of canonicity with it. Examples of a minor criticism already in existence might possibly include a text such as Charles Olson's *Call Me Ishmael*, long recognized as simultaneously something less and more than criticism. Still, the budding theory of a minor literature appears to risk a spiralling *reductio*, displacing, even though they may be culturally determined, the basic questions of association and disparity and relation. Fortunately, my project does not extend to this point, since its desire is to sketch an interface where the "minor" comments upon the "major."

An impulse to concentrate upon James's "neglected" works is of course not original with me—I am reminded immediately of the recent work of Susanne Kappeler, John Carlos Rowe and Allon White.[14] And yet, the near unanimity of selection among these efforts cannot pass without comment. The joint shift of critical focus to such texts as "The Aspern Papers," *The Sacred Fount* and *The Ivory Tower*—where there are simply too many "unread letters," "mirrors" and "doubles" to pass up—tends toward the establishment of an alternative canon, whose members are more flexibly amenable to their employment as confirmations of the rapidly ossifying dictates of fashionable critical methodologies. Such a remark as this is not, however, an indictment of specific critical efforts, but a reflection on the remarkable power of canons to reassert themselves, despite the admonitions of Michel Foucault or Roland Barthes, or our attempts to heed them. My selection of James's neglected texts, to the extent that it avoids the construction of an alternative canon, does so primarily through the machinery of chance. My method is that of close reading, bordering on the microscopic, coupled with a respect for the dimensions of intertextuality, particularly as regards the connection between the short stories and the Notebooks.

What emerges from these readings is a series of reflections on some of Henry James's more obscure short stories, stories that would hazard a differing, contrary relation to the idea of the Master. Describing the contours of that relation will be the task of the succeeding chapters, though it should be noted here that the difficulties of various narrative modes will often prove to be figural, along with the powerful mechanisms of humor and irony. It should be noted as well that a certain amount of slippage among the critical terms employed here was, it seemed to me, a necessary risk: the phenomenon I have chosen to label "mastery" in this introduction—a choice based wholly on familiarity—will variously emerge in these texts as "authority," "authorship," "mastery," "control," "law," and otherwise. It would have been far easier, and far more consistent, to collapse all these admittedly vague terms into a single univocal label—"mastery," perhaps—but aside from considerations of accuracy with regard to the usage in the texts themselves, it is precisely this homogenizing unity of definition which is a chief attribute of the "mastery" these texts seek to resist. If "authorship" and "authority" stand in my text in an uneasy and ambivalent alliance, much will have been gained.

We have seen that what makes "The Figure in the Carpet" a master-text is that it implicitly authorizes the act of interpretation, through its enactment of a relation of master to reader that provides the space for interpretation, the corrections of an infinitely repeating critical discourse. And the ability to comment on the commentary is also authorized: it inheres in the structure of the relation, the aura of power—empty and horrible—that is the author's voice. The contrast to this would be a text that somehow limits the power of the interpreter—but how can this be? Our impulse in such a case is to find a source of failure—that is, either the text is not sufficiently well executed or its reader is not sufficiently perceptive to allow it to have "perpetual modernity." But if we discard the knee-jerk appeal to "quality," we find that such texts do indeed exist, buried in the collection of Henry James's short fictions. What we encounter in these stories is that the image of the relation between Vereker and the narrator of "The Figure in the Carpet," our relation to Henry James the Master, is extended to us, and then withdrawn, criticized or exploded. This movement also resembles that portion of "The Figure in the Carpet" I previously isolated—Corvick and Erme as the cancellation of opposites, the perfect supplement that negates the need to speak further. Despite our best efforts, the narrator of that story occupies our place and we his, regardless of the way we may judge him, in that the infinity of spiraling motion is maintained. For Corvick and Erme, however, after the "sharing" of Vereker's secret, there is no need to talk—their possession of each other eclipses Vereker as an individuated, and opposing, force. The stories that we will investigate here offer, in different forms, the same silence, in a presentation of the Master that would encourage our speaking back to him, and the simultaneous cancellation of his place, his removal, so that there is nothing to speak of or to. The only way to respond, then, is to sketch out this disjunction, the places and the moments when the Master relents.

Two difficulties persist, however—both trenchant, both on the order of paradox. First, such a project as this one would seem to lay claim to a certain measure of originality: by the redirection of interpretative energies to those texts which are outside of or (worse) in opposition to the traditions of canonical authority, one would apparently stand accused of a novel approach to an established subject, or even of the attempted subversion of that subject's authoritative stature. As attractive as these possibilities may be, they are unfortunately not the case. In addition to the reinforcement of canonical authority inherent in its crystallization, even as an object of attack, it is essential to recognize that, while such a redirection takes as its object the marginal or the rejected, the method of that redirection is itself firmly within the mainstream of institutionalized criticism. In other words, the establishment in my text of an entrenched critical tradition, only to depart from it, is a time-honored critical maneuver, a subversion in name only that is readily assimilable into the parameters of authoritarian critical discourse. What is canonically invalid is thus recuperated through what is hermeneutically valid—a consideration doubly emphasized by the fact that my text originally appeared in the form of a doctoral dissertation, and was hardly disinterested in the institutionalized judgments of competency attendant thereto.[15] The notion of originality, taken even as a qualified epithet, is, therefore, if not illusory, then at least powerfully compromised.

The second point of difficulty is even more profoundly paradoxical. As with most introductions, what appears first was written last, and as my own text begins to slip from my fingers I am faced with the question of my own intention, and of the effect I have sought to produce. The following pages speak of unfair exclusion, and of retrieval—the implication would seem to be that I advise the recovery of these marginal works from the oblivion in which they languish, through their rereading and reevaluation. And yet, to the extent that my investigations may provoke further thought and discussion, the works themselves are exposed to the danger of being recuperated into the Jamesian canon, and with this recuperation comes the necessary loss of the neglected status which accounts in large part for their particular charm. I share with Henry James his affinity for these outsiders, "standing wistful but excluded," and am hesitant to exchange for them the indignity of rejection for the patronage of acceptance. As Frank Kermode has stated,

> Opinion is the great canon-maker, and you can't have privileged insiders without creating outsiders, apocrypha. The attention of those learned (but still opinionated) communities who assume responsibility for the continuance and modernity of the canon is naturally fixed on the insiders, and the others are allowed to fall under the rule of time, to become merely historical. For one reason or another they may continue to exist, but because the attention they attract is sporadic and relatively unengaged, their state is at best that of half-life; they too are the victims of chance and opinion. Continuity of attention and interpretation, denied to them, is reserved for the canonical.[16]

I have no solution for this dilemma, short of insuring a refusal of community by asking my reader to stop reading now—an option I am naturally reluctant to exercise. Instead, I will simply join these texts in their subjection to the rule of time, and proceed in a few pleasant if discontinuous moments of engagement.

2

Addressing "A Bundle of Letters": The Hazard of Authority

While weathering an unusually violent Parisian snowstorm in the autumn of 1879, Henry James wrote, "in a single long session and, the temperature apart, at a 'heat,'" his much neglected tale "A Bundle of Letters." It was, he tells us, the production of "a deep concentration, an unusual straightness of labour."[1] In the century that has passed since that day, what scant critical attention this tale has received has been, if not dismissive, then at best deprecatory.[2] Despite James's later decision to include "A Bundle of Letters" in the New York Edition, with the resulting imprimatur that that inclusion implies, this tale is seen as quaint, trivial—a rather undistinguished example of an early Jamesian motif. Tony Tanner writes: "Following the success of this story ['Daisy Miller'] James rushed out a series of stories on the international theme —'The Pension Beaurepas,' 'An International Episode,' 'A Bundle of Letters,' 'The Point of View.' These are not stories so much as vehicles for his own mixed attitudes towards Europe and America."[3]

Tanner's comment is typical, in several respects. "A Bundle of Letters" is seen as a largely unrealized execution of a theme treated more deftly elsewhere; it is confused, the reflection of "mixed attitudes." But what is most interesting here is the attempt to classify this work as something other than what it appears to be: it is not so much a "story" as a "vehicle." Cornelia Pulsifer Kelley, in *The Early Development of Henry James,* makes the same distinction, characterizing it as a "study" rather than a "story."[4]

To a degree, these criticisms are correct. "A Bundle of Letters" is not a "story," in the sense that a story must conform to previously determined rules and expectations. It is not a story precisely because James plays with and around the notion of authoritative forms and the discourse that enacts them. "A Bundle of Letters" is incomplete, but not because it is "inconsequential," because "nothing happens."[5] It is incomplete because, while playing precisely at the interface between these rules of authoritative discourse and a sense of innocent, unlettered speech, James has created a text with a hole in it—a hole through which the reader will more than likely slip. Although it may be true that James intended to capitalize on his newly recognized position as "the fictional historian of 'the American girl,'"[6] "A Bundle of Letters" nonetheless captures a striking presentation—if only an ironic, deflected one—of ideas and themes that will recur repeatedly throughout James's work. This singleness of concentration, this "heat," produced an authentic example of Jamesian art.

I

The title of "A Bundle of Letters" reflects in large measure the construction of this tale, which consists of nine letters written by the various inhabitants of a Parisian pension who have gathered there for the purpose of polishing their French conversation. The letters are in a "bundle," as their arrangement seems somewhat haphazard on the first reading—it is difficult to discern a clear pattern to their appearance. Yet such a pattern does exist, brought about by James's proportionately balanced exposition of the international theme. While the story consists of nine letters, the letters are written by only six characters—three Americans and three Europeans. The American contingent is comprised of Miranda Hope, an independent young woman from Bangor, Maine, who is making the "grand tour" unescorted (and who occupies the place of central character if only because of her authorship of four of the letters); Violet Ray, a money- and status-conscious New York socialite; and Louis Leverett, a self-professed Bostonian esthete. Each of the Americans represents, both through their different places of origin and their disparate attitudes and concerns, a distinct yet familiar Jamesian "type." The Europeans are likewise distinguished one from the other by nationality and social rank: Evelyn Vane serves as a representative of the lesser English nobility; Leon Verdier, the Frenchman, combines his position as a somewhat dubious tutor of French with a penchant for seduction; and the German Rudolf Staub, professor and man of science, exercises his critical faculties on the "subjects" arrayed before him. James's choice of the epistolary form affords him the well-known virtue of that technique, "the ability to present a rounded picture of an event by recording it from several contrasting points of view."[7]

By avoiding obvious authorial intrusion, and by opposing a set of three different Americans with a set of three different Europeans, James presents us with a singularly even-handed portrayal of the international theme: no one character can be said to be favored over another; each has his own attractions and follies. On the other hand, to view "A Bundle of Letters" solely from this perspective results in a curiously static reading. The very qualities that produce a balanced presentation produce as well no resolution, for there is no real plot to resolve: James's multiple points of view have led him into a kind of narrative cul-de-sac, where the "rounded picture" contains no "event." Thus, if this story is to be regarded as anything more than a "study," it must be read on another basis than that of the international theme.

It is here that it must be noted, despite the apparent stress on the encounter of American with European, and the widely divergent points of view thereby engendered, that the characters in "A Bundle of Letters" have all assembled for a common purpose—that of "learning the language." Further, for each of them, learning the language is not an end in itself, as it involves the acquisition of a base of power through a command of the language, and through the control that that command represents. Evelyn Vane's brother Harold studies to pass his impending "exams"; Violet has come to work on her "verbs" (an appropriate area of weakness for someone already so enmeshed in things and the nouns that name them); Dr. Staub comes in furtherance of his political and ideological goals; Leverett seeks the somewhat less dangerous but no less seductive realization of the ideology of the esthete; and Miranda Hope, New England suffragette and American *naïve extraordinaire,* comes to learn French for the purpose of self-realization, to "see it for herself," as it were.

It is Miranda on whom our gaze comes to rest, in her role as central character and main correspondent. And at the very outset, Miranda's use of language in her letters home can be seen to indicate not communication but *transaction.* The second paragraph of her initial letter contains the first of a series of mentions of her erstwhile Bangor beau William Platt. While her Plattitudes can obviously be read as the expected and appropriate coquetries of a girl, they are significant in that they signal clearly and repeatedly that her "relation" with Platt must be based on a transaction. She tells her mother that she will not write a letter directly to him because "if he wants one for himself, he has got to write to me first. Let him write to me first, and then I will see about answering him."[8] The litany of indirect address to Platt culminates with her command to "tell William Platt I don't care what he does" (*BL,* 434). This is of course the very opposite of the truth—her repeated references to him demonstrate that—but while it is opposite, it is not ironic, because Miranda lacks the distance and play necessary for the ironic reversal. It is intended merely as a challenge, a stimulus designed to evoke a desired response. Her references to Platt are reminiscent of Roland Barthes's description of the lover's discourse in the proffering of the *I- love-you,* which must be regarded "not as a symptom but as an action."[9] The one who speaks *I-love-you* says to the other: "I speak so that you may answer, and the scrupulous form (the letter) of the answer will assume an effective value, in the manner of a formula. Hence it is not enough that the other should answer me with a mere signified, however positive (*'So do I'*): the addressed subject must take the responsibility of formulating, of proffering the *I-love-you* which I extend."[10] The Barthesian lover, through the utterance of the gestural *I-love-you,* enacts a discourse that stands against language, that resists the forces of dissuasion and analysis inherent there. Miranda, however, seeks entry *into* a language, and consequently her circumlocutions toward Platt devolve back into the limits of the discourse of authority and acquisition: she does not offer a gift in an act of speaking, but seeks instead to establish an exchange of letters, to strike a bargain within the mediate realm of writing. Miranda's deal with Platt marks the first step in her acquisition of the discourse of power, because

> the one who does not say *I-love-you* (between whose lips *I-love-you* is reluctant to pass) is condemned to emit the many uncertain, doubting, greedy signs of love, its indices, its "proofs": gestures, looks, sighs, allusions, ellipses: he must let himself be *interpreted*; he is dominated by the reactive occasion of love's signs, exiled into the servile world of language *in that he does not say everything*.[11]

Her relation with Platt reflects not a desire to proffer, but to profit.

The linguistic interplay with the absent Platt is but one instance of Miranda's employment of language as an instrument of transaction and appropriation. Though she confides to her mother that the theater is a poor teacher of the language, because of the "many vulgar expressions which it is unnecessary to learn" (*BL*, 431), it is at the theater that she first happens upon the idea of going to the pension.

> I heard two gentlemen talking behind me. It was between the acts, and I couldn't help listening to what they said. They were talking English, but I guess they were Americans.
> "Well," said one of them, "it all depends on what you are after. I'm after French; that's what I'm after."
> "Well," said the other, "I'm after Art."
> "Well," said the first, "I'm after Art too; but I'm after French most." (*BL*, 432)[12]

While these two Americans are, in their rapacious pursuit of the spoils of Europe, indicative of an all too familiar Jamesian type, it ought not be assumed that Miranda is either immune to their attitude, or somehow the passive recorder of it. She acquires from them the notion of going to live with a French family in order to "get" French, and she does so through a small theft, an act of eavesdropping on the private conversation of another. In the same letter, when she describes her room at the pension, she does so not so much with adjectives, but with a catalogue of its furnishings, a list of her temporary "possessions": it is "a very pretty little room—without any carpet, but with seven mirrors, two clocks, and five curtains" (*BL*, 434).

This tendency to employ language as a medium of acquisition reaches its apotheosis in Verdier, the leering seducer, and Staub, the proto-fascist. Distinguished from their fellow correspondents by their already having achieved a certain facility with the modes of authoritative discourse, they signal the clearest demonstration of the notion that learning the language is not a goal in itself, but a means through which one is able to acquire further; and, in these two instance, the acquisition is not of things or ideas, but of *people,* as objects. The styles of their respective letters are revelatory in this regard. Verdier's letter might be said to introduce the discourse of the nudge, as it is replete with the insinuations and innuendoes of the womanizer's knowing wink. It is especially noteworthy that when French—Miranda's goal—actually emerges in this story, it comes as a reflection back upon her: "*elle ne demande qu'à se laisser aller*"; "*elle brûle ses vaisseux celle-la*" (*BL*, 458). Staub, on the other hand, combines the jargon of the academy with that of the totalitarian propagandist. He dismisses Verdier as a kind of simian "homunculus," an example of the French as subhuman species. Admittedly, this rejection seems appropriate for one of the ideological bent of Staub, who is chillingly rendered as the ancestor of the Nietzschean *übermensch* and the brownshirts. But it is strange and oddly funny to realize that James's irony allows us to perceive this response in two ways. It is first a reaction to the presence of the opposite, and its discourse, since Verdier, a Frenchman *and* an irrational, sexual "animal," is everything that Staub hates. But it is also a reaction to the presence of a kindred spirit, for in their common use of the technique of disparagement, the Prussian intellectual and the French seducer are revealed to share a common goal—the power of conquest.

II

Miranda is a writer, of sorts: she is responsible for four of the nine letters which comprise the bundle, and is keeping a "most *exhaustive* journal" which will ostensibly chronicle her European tour for the audience in Bangor. But it is not so much the writing that Miranda does that is of interest here—rather, it is the writing she does *not* do.

Intent on seeking out a suitable French family with which to study, Miranda is directed to the pension by the bookkeeper at her hotel, a woman whose distinguishing mark is the ominous one of being clothed entirely in black. Of this lady in black, Miranda writes:

> She has given me a great deal of information about the position of woman in France, and much of it is very encouraging. But she has told me at the same time some things that I should not like to write to you (I am hesitating even about putting them into my journal). . . . I assure you they appear to talk about things here that we never think of mentioning at Bangor, or even of thinking about. (*BL*, 429–30)

What these "things" are we are never told: Miranda is at least true to her word. But this is the first hint that James gives that things may not be all that they seem at the pension run by Madame Maisonrouge.

The question of what can be said, of censorship, derives primarily from questions of what society demands. In pondering it, Miranda, as student of the language, reflects on the difference between conversation in Paris and that in Bangor:

> The conversation in the parlor . . . is often remarkably brilliant, and I often wish that you, or some of the Bangor folks, could be there to enjoy it. Even though you couldn't understand it I think you would like to hear the way they go on; they seem to express so much. I sometimes think that at Bangor they don't express enough (but it seems as if over there, there was less to express). It seems as if, at Bangor, there were things that folks never *tried* to say; but here, I have learned from studying French that you have no idea what you *can* say, before you try. (*BL,* 445–46)

We find Miranda slowly beginning to evidence the realization that language exists not merely as a channel for the communication of preconceived notions, but functions also as a creative source of thought: much of what she thinks and feels is not operated upon *by* language, but is discovered and made real only *through* it. This idea is expanded upon in her next paragraph, as she muses over the treatment she receives at the hands of Violet Ray:

> But it seems as if she didn't want to recognise me, or associate with me; as if she wanted to make a difference between us. It is like people they call "haughty" in books. I have never seen any one like that before—any one that wanted to make a difference; and at first I was right down interested, she seemed to me so like a proud young lady in a novel. I kept saying to myself all day, "haughty, haughty," and I wished she would keep on so. (*BL,* 446)

Here, Miranda reacts to her rejection, and resolves her puzzlement, at least temporarily, by explaining away Violet's behavior as "haughty." The act of describing a person and her conduct becomes an act of labeling, with the label being taken from a received set of prearranged codes: novels. Of course, it is not unusual for the young and innocent to deal with new experiences on the basis of old ones, or to explain the mystifying in terms of the understood. But Miranda's operation of understanding here involves the overlay of a text onto the field of "real life": the set of experiences she uses—the novels—are received, "authorized" texts, with their own set of codes entailing their own set of responses. Note here as well the persistent appearance of colloquialisms in Miranda's letters: "right down interested" and "right down curious" must be replaced by the accepted formulae of authoritative utterance if the entrance into the sphere of authoritative power is to be made. Admission into "society"—even a hostile (Violet), or exploitative (Verdier), or insipid (Leverett) society—for the *naïf,* is a matter of initiation into the appropriate texts, and into the process of textualizing.

With her growing awareness that language functions not as a passive vehicle of communication but as a socially authorized discourse entailing methods of control, Miranda's attention is shifted to the complicated issue of style. "Even though you couldn't understand it I think you would like to hear the way they go on," she tells her mother, for it is no longer the content of the message but the nature of the message itself that has become crucial. We begin to witness in Miranda the dawning of the esthetic perspective, or perhaps something altogether more disconcerting.

Miranda's admiration of the Vanes is unequivocal, and bases itself on just this criterion: "I do love their way of speaking, and sometimes I feel almost as if it would be right to give up trying to learn French, and just try to learn to speak our own tongue as these English speak it. It isn't the things they say so much, though these are often rather curious, but it is in the way they pronounce, and the sweetness of their voice" (*BL,* 448). But if her praise is unequivocal, her expression of it is not: an appreciation of the "sweetness" of a voice is by definition a matter of "taste." Miranda's immersion in the language is no longer simply a matter of acquiring nouns and verbs, but has become a question of her ability to make discriminations of quality. Even though she dislikes the Englishman for his conservatism and bemused sexism, and is likewise aware at some level of his sister's radiant vacuity, she cannot help but admire their style. "General culture," as she puts it, involves not a breaking through but an elimination of the barriers between them, an effort to make the representatives of authority "recognize me, or associate with me."

It is to penetrate these mysteries that Miranda goes to the home of Madame Maisonrouge, there to hire Verdier as her tutor. We are soon to realize, from Verdier's letter, the implications of the term "extra private lessons"—that it indicates not merely private lessons that are extra, but "lessons" that are "extra-private." As with the lady in black, Miranda confides to her mother that Verdier's discourse is not for the page: "He converses with great fluency, and I feel as if I should really gain from him. He is remarkably handsome, and extremely polite—paying a great many compliments, which, I am afraid, are not always *sincere*. When I return to Bangor I will tell you some of the things he has said to me. I think you will consider them extremely curious, and very beautiful *in their way*" (*BL,* 445). The passages James italicized point out the central issue here: the determination of the truth that may or may not lie in any particular utterance—the question of "sincerity"—is supplanted by the invocation of different "ways" of speaking. At the beginning of this letter, Miranda tells her mother not to worry about not having heard from her sooner, as she isn't in any trouble, but if she *were* in trouble, she would not write to tell of it, either. This charming contradiction underscores Miranda's essential naivete and youth, but placed as it is at the head of a lengthy if ill-defined rumination on the matter of style, it serves as an ironic warning of things to come, and of Miranda's growing awareness of her own ability to dissemble. Verdier's seductive phrases cannot or will not be written: they are to be communicated, if at all, only in person, upon her return to Bangor. The introduction of Verdier announces the beginning of the lie: the sincerity of his words is doubted, then excused on the basis of their being of a different "way." But her contextualization of Verdier's discourse still does not give Miranda sufficient cause to avoid excluding examples of it from her letter, in an act of censorship that raises a most telling point. Ordinarily, one would think that the written text necessitates, even creates, an author, an authoritative voice that guarantees the veracity of that text, if only provisionally; while speech, conversely, allows for the hedging and revision of play. Thus, it might be assumed that Verdier's speech is too "ambiguous" for inclusion in the written text—it would not survive the transition. But the discourse of the seducer, while circuitous in its reference, is never so in its motives or its goal, as is made abundantly clear in Verdier's letter: there is no hedging there. It would seem then that, in "A Bundle of Letters," the working out of the question of desire, even on the level of sexual innuendo, is more ambiguous in the written text, so that all of Miranda's "connections" with her *own* desire—the woman in black, Verdier, Madame Maisonrouge—are unable to be translated into *her* letters. Though Miranda may be able to say that "I feel really as if I should gain all I desire" (*BL*, 430), all that she desires cannot be named.

III

In his portrait of Louis Leverett, James allows himself the liberty to lampoon the "type" of the consumptive esthete with the sort of broad brush rarely found in his later fiction. Leverett's reluctance to offend the illustrious "West Cedar Street circle" or the frumpy, disinterested "Johnsons" points up the paucity of the "aesthetic" viewpoint he espouses with such ineffectual fervor. At the same time, Leverett is made to speak what have become some of the central canons of Jamesian criticism. It is Leverett, after all, who tells his friend Harvard Trement that "the great thing is to *live*" (*BL*, 441), a phrase that will echo throughout James's later work, most notably from the mouth of Lambert Strether in *The Ambassadors*. It is interesting to speculate that James's great themes were already before him in 1879, and find their way into this text, if only in the cloak of irony. While he congratulates himself for taking up residence "in a French family, in a real Parisian house," in order to "see something of *real French life*" (*BL*, 440–41), Leverett is as far from finding the "real" French as is Miranda. If such a dissipated, fatuous fool is allowed to spout "the important thing is to *live*," not only the speaker but the contents of his speech must be called into question. Can James himself have regarded so unambiguously the advice of one such as Leverett when he says: "I like to do everything frankly, freely, *naïvement, au grand jour*. That is the great thing—to be free, to be frank, to be *naïf*. Doesn't Matthew Arnold say that somewhere—or is it Swinburne, or Pater?" (*BL*, 440).

Leverett's letter is the fourth in the bundle. The first two, from Miranda to her mother, may be taken as one—they set forth the particulars of her presence in the house of Madame Maisonrouge. The third letter, that of Violet Ray, provides counterpoint—we begin to see the same incidents, circumstances and people described in a wholly different way, tinged with the expected affectations of the New York society girl. It is with the fourth letter, Leverett's, that the reader begins to realize fully that things are not quite what they seem. While Miranda regards her surroundings with a general acceptance of appearances, Violet begins to call into question the legitimacy and decorum of the whole enterprise, while Leverett provides a third, mediated view. With Leverett's letter, we find ourselves no longer trying to determine the true status of Mme. Maisonrouge, and whether her operation is shady or not, but instead we are brought up against the question of how to determine the veracity of any of the letter writers—whether we can trust, or assign authority to, any of what we read. Miranda regards the pension and its occupants from the point of view of Yankee economy and efficiency; Violet sees in it the dissolute and somewhat disgraceful sham of a woman of questionable virtue; Leverett sees it as the paradigm of his beloved Parisian atmosphere. What the truth is can no longer be determined: each of the three reads the surroundings through the glass of his or her own pre- and mis-conceptions. The usual presence of an authoritative narrator is replaced, subsumed by a collection of competing versions, none altogether true or altogether false—perhaps. What is called into question here is not just the circumspection of three characters who are in a sense truly "naive," but the issue of authoritative textuality: how to believe what we read.

Of special interest here is the allegorical quality of the characters' names. Our heroine is Miranda Hope;[13] Louis *Leverett* would truly arise, if he could; Leon *Verdier* indeed tends the verdure, and assists the growing things; and of course Madame *Maisonrouge* runs a house that is perhaps very red indeed. In the otherwise empty letter of Evelyn *Vane* (who, in her vanity, goes which way the wind blows), James offers us a splendid joke in the anecdote of Lady *Battledown* paying her governesses £5 more a year to change their names to Johnson, as "they shouldn't have a nicer name than the family" (*BL,* 453). The names are clever, true, but they are so patently significant that they issue a challenge to the reader to look beyond mere allegory. As we have seen that the determination of whether Madame Maisonrouge runs a red house is itself undermined by the inability of the separate narrators to reach an authoritative consensus, so we the readers must look beyond the apparent allegorical significances of the names of those narrators. In a surprising show of modernism, James assumes the flatly significant allegory not for the sake of descriptive labelling, but in order to draw attention to such a simplistic act of authoritative significance, and whether it is possible at all.

The anecdote of Lady Battledown is indeed humorous: it presents us with the foolishness and self-importance of the titled aristocracy in a bit of homely burlesque. But it must be remembered that the overriding feature of humor resides in its relation to authority. Humor allows us to take an otherwise inescapable circumstance, an instance of pain created and sustained by the force of unalterable authority, and deflect that authority for a moment, placing in its stead the momentary forgiveness and release of the joke.[14] While the story of Lady Battledown is a joke, it is a *good* joke because it masks the awful truth of a system that would permit and even encourage such an action as hers. Lady Battledown is in fact capable of changing the names and therein altering the identities of those in her employ—the existing set of social rules, the power of the realm of authoritative discourse, makes possible the subjugation of those without it through the systematic control of their names.[15] As Miranda learns French to acquire the culture, to enter into the modes of discourse that reflect real power, those modes begin to reveal themselves to the reader not merely as linguistic conventions and societal norms, but as the methods and means of controlling the process of signification, and thereby of determining meaning and truth. Each of the narrators learns the "language" to some extent, but their respective abilities to manipulate these modes of control remain incomplete. That is to say, from the privileged point of view of the reader, we can see where they contradict each other, and where the limited apprehension of one character is manifested in contrast with that of another. Therefore, to assign veracity, or truthfulness, to any particular narrative over the others, or even to parts of some of the narratives over other parts, is to engage in an arbitrary and unwarranted assignation of authority, not a discovery of a preordained, dependable authoritative statement hidden somewhere in the text. We do not reveal the concealed here—if we try, we get nowhere we can trust.

IV

The last letter of the nine comprising the bundle is again from Miranda to her mother. In it we find the conclusion of the episode at the pension, and her intention to move on to "fresh experiences." It would appear at first glance that very little has been resolved in this story, and that the last letter does little to explain the questions raised by the previous eight. This is to be expected in a story that holds before us throughout the difficulty of obtaining authoritative resolution to the problems of literary statement. Yet the investigations that James has begun in the preceding eight letters do find a further exposition in the last letter, and to a surprising end.

On one level, "A Bundle of Letters" can be read as an evenly weighted presentation of the international theme—three Americans square off against three Europeans. But only one of these Americans—Miranda Hope—commands our attention. Her letters, placed as they are at the beginning, middle and end of this tale, do not so much reflect her membership in the American faction as constitute the signposts of the successive stages of her European education. In her initiation into the discourse of authority, Miranda is taught a series of separate "language" lessons by each of the European correspondents. From Evelyn Vane she receives a lesson on the subject of style, coupled with instruction on the matter of economic oppression effected by the systematic application of stylistic modes. Verdier teaches her metaphor, and as he exposes her to the lie and to innuendo, Miranda learns to communicate her experience through a technique of re-presentation that makes room for the expression of desire in the space of the unsaid. Staub lectures her on rhetoric, and prepares her to expand the scope of her incipient control from the level of the individual to that of whole populations. In a series of graduated steps, the novice learns to contain what are actually robbery, rape, and murder within the mediate confines of authoritative discourse, and thereby to enter "general culture." By the time of her arrival at the last letter, the reader must look to the changes these lessons will have produced in Miranda—changes that will manifest themselves in how she writes.

In some respects, Miranda appears to have changed very little. She accepts wholesale Violet's explanation that their initial misunderstanding was merely the result of a grammatical misstatement, without reflecting on the possibility of innocence with regard to such a question. She seems as gullible as ever, describing Staub as "more interesting, the more you know him"; she "could fairly drink in his ideas" (*BL*, 465). And yet, the innocent Yankee vulgarity that characterized Miranda in her first letter has been tempered somewhat, by something unexplained. Although her ingenuous remarks persist, Miranda also writes of Verdier as one "from whom I have gained more than I ever expected (in six weeks), and with whom I have promised to *correspond*. So you can imagine me dashing off the most correct French letters; and, if you don't believe it, I will keep the rough draft to show you when I go back" (*BL*, 465). In Verdier's letter, we are faced with the question of whether his attempts at seduction will succeed— whether he will bring his "lessons" to their intended conclusion—and the intervening letter of Staub only serves to heighten the suspense through the delay of an answer. In the last letter, Miranda naturally does not write that he has so succeeded, but to the jaundiced eye a number of significant traces are visible. She has gained more than she expected; she has promised to *correspond*. The connotations of "correspondence" are familiar to readers of the epistolary form; here, the implication is driven home doubly by the italicization of that word, echoing that of the "*extra private lessons*." Showing her letters (now in French) only when she gets back refers once again to difficulties in translating the ambiguous, and it is here that the notion of a "draft" is brought forth. A draft implies a final copy—the revised and corrected version of an edited text. Since the edited text reflects conformity to the accepted rules of a discourse, Miranda has, it would seem, mastered the notion of learning the language as an issue of control—she has learned "French."

Now, the incident with Violet becomes less innocent in its implications. While it may be true that Miranda remains as naive as ever with regard to Violet's true feelings, while she may be unable to perceive that their differences run far deeper than a grammatical flub, it is her ability to perceive the flub, the mistake, and the humor of it, that distinguishes Miranda from our first glimpse of her. Recognizing the mistake requires newly acquired knowledge of the rules of the language; seeing the humor implies mastery of those rules.

"Tell William Platt his letter has come. I knew he would have to write, and I was bound I would make him!" (*BL*, 465). The transaction between Miranda and the absent Platt is completed, though not finished, by his entry into the cycle of correspondence. Miranda's mastery of the "language" has granted her the power to control the flow of discourse, to enter into the relations of power implied in correspondence, in writing. She says she was "bound" she would make him, and she did.

Most important in this regard is a detail of James's text that almost escapes attention—the tiniest of implications, but therefore of the greatest significance. Miranda's first letter is dated September 5, the second on the sixteenth, and the third on the twenty-sixth. The picture is that of the dutiful daughter, writing to her mother every ten days or so, and making the required report. The last letter is dated October 22, and follows her third by a gap of 26 days, fully two and one-half times as long as is usual. The "resolution" of "A Bundle of Letters," the answer to the reader's questions, is contained in a chronological hole in the text that the reader must fill. One must hesitate to assign much weight to such an apparently trivial detail as the dates of the letters, but for an author whose closest skirmish with the actuality of sexual desire is the breaking of the Golden Bowl—the physical sign of the metaphor of the possibility of the opportunity for sexual relations—the significance of such a detail is manifest. When Miranda told her mother that she would not write if anything were wrong, she spoke truly.

Allon White, among others, has noted the recurrent tendency in Jamesian narratives to hide such potentially hazardous moments: "Again and again, James returned to the story of a compromised and compromising seduction, a passion forced into deviousness. The passion is central to the story, it is the energy which drives the narrative, but it is unacknowledged as such and 'the scene of seduction' . . . which is the pivotal moment of this narrative, remains as concealed as possible."[16] However, White goes on to ascribe this quality primarily to James's later novels, distinguishing them from those earlier works where the shock of assault on the sensibility or person of an innocent is more "clearly felt" by the reader. His latter point would be true if James's work were limited to the accepted and selected few—but here we find the same technique of concealment in a tale that directly follows "Daisy Miller," and purports to mimic its formula. Perhaps the tendency to what White calls "obscurity" is present even this early—but the admission of it would certainly make a hash of the lovely divisions of early, middle and late James.

Of course, we cannot be certain that Miranda has in fact been seduced. We cannot expect the authority to make such a pronouncement in a story that unhinges, that mocks, "author-ity." But it is just that play with narrative authority, with a trustworthy statement—that subtle and recurrent calling into question of the motives and mechanisms of such statements—that makes it unnecessary to know for certain the "true" result. In James, we find a lack of necessity for a clear-cut reference to sexual liaison—it is sufficient that the possibility exists, that the competing traces are there. In "A Bundle of Letters," the gap in the text, the innuendo, and the presence of a possibílity are enough; for what is required in James is not proof positive, but the absence of proof negative—a question of determination on the basis of the "not-un" adjectival formula.

Miranda enters this story to some extent "unlettered." She lacks not only French, but grammatically correct English: note again the habitual Yankee colloquialisms that characterize her letters. But, in comparing the last line of her first letter with that of her last letter, we find that "Dear mother, my money holds out very well, and it *is* real interesting" (*BL*, 430) has become "Dearest mother, my money holds out, and it *is* most interesting" (*BL*, 465). While the form remains essentially the same, and Miranda (or her money) is still gathering interest, it is important to note what has changed: "Dear mother" has been altered to the more formal and affected "Dearest mother," and the colloquial "real interesting" has given way to the proper "most interesting." By the time of the ninth and last letter, the reader must be intrigued with whether or not Miranda—not as virgin, but as token of American virginity—will emerge unscathed: will the sign be saved? We find that she has indeed emerged intact, but altered: she does not greet her initiation with the histrionic breakdown of her kinswoman and fellow scribbler Clarissa, but she is changed nonetheless. The edges have been smoothed; the untamed American has entered society, and learned to speak French.

V

The title of "A Bundle of Letters" refers obviously to the nine missives that make up this story. But letters are also alphabetic characters, a "bundle" of individual signifiers that by themselves and in isolation mean nothing. It is only by the arrangement of these signifiers that we acquire meaning, and these arrangements are both arbitrary and rigidly controlled. That is to say, there is no underlying reason as to why certain arrangements of "letters" signify what they do, but, given the existence of those arbitrary arrangements, their control and use becomes rigidly prescribed, so that learning the language involves a grounding in the rules and patterns of significations that both reflect and signal entry into the matrix of power that backs that language.

In his title, James has presented us with the dynamic of a system of signification that preserves its arbitrary qualities within a grid of determination—the determination of "true" meaning is seen as a function of the arbitrary. While the letters are random, contained in a "bundle" that implies haphazard collection, they are also controlled by a system of authoritative discourse. By throwing his reader into the interface between *what* his text means and *how* it means, by constructing a system of authoritative textuality within a framework that systematically deconstructs that very system, James manages, at least tentatively, at least conditionally, to maintain the ambiguity that stands outside authority. We are granted the room to be unsure, to question and requestion, to wonder.

Shattered Notions of Mastery: "Glasses"

"Glasses" first appeared in the *Atlantic Monthly* in February of 1896. In this tale, James presents us with an unnamed narrator—a portrait painter whose comparative lack of circumspection is promptly telegraphed to the reader, if only by his repeated gratuitous remarks about long-nosed Jews. This narrator tells the story of the beautiful but ill-fated Flora Saunt, a sort of composite Daisy Miller/Milly Theale, but neither so naive as the former nor static as the latter. Though lacking an attractive figure, Flora possesses a face so beautiful that she charms all those who come in contact with her. Our narrator meanwhile learns, through Flora's outspoken friend Mrs. Meldrum, that Flora's beautiful eyes will soon fail her completely unless she consents to wear a particularly hideous pair of eyeglasses much like Mrs. Meldrum's own, with huge convex lenses and a horizontal bar running across them. This remedy is rejected by Flora, however, whose perfect face is her only real chance to make a rich and successful marriage. The power of this face is revealed only when a portrait our narrator paints of it provokes the admiration of an ugly and rather undistinguished Englishman named Geoffrey Dawling, whose offer of marriage Flora turns down, preferring to pursue a match with the more handsomely appointed Lord Iffield. But when the nobleman learns of Flora's fatal flaw, in a scene the narrator secretly witnesses, the intended marriage is called off. Crushed, Flora goes to live with Mrs. Meldrum and begins to wear the loathsome spectacles. After a lapse of several years, our narrator returns from America to discover by chance the revivified Flora, more beautiful than ever, bedecked in jewels and without her glasses. He rushes to join her in her box at the opera, and there is horrified to learn that she has regained her beauty only at the cost of her eyes: married at last to the once-spurned Dawling, she is now totally blind.

This curiously haunting tale was collected in the volume James entitled *Embarrassments,* along with "The Figure in the Carpet," "The Next Time" and "The Way It Came." And the label "embarrassment" seems to have stuck: this story has largely eluded anthologists and critics alike, with the few critical appraisals it has received ranging from Granville H. Jones's classification of it as a study in grotesquery, to Adeline Tintner's unfortunate hypothesis that the tale is little more than a cleverly devised plagiarism of Poe's "The Spectacles."[1] One might contend that this story is ultimately a failure, that its rather trite ending lacks punch or that it too frequently lapses into melodrama. But these criticisms, even if well founded, do not go far enough in explaining its exclusion from the Jamesian canon. I would contend, on the contrary, that "Glasses" has earned its neglected status through its tacit undermining of the very basis on which a determination of canonicity rests: the figure of the Master that permeates our reading of Henry James. This is not to say that the criticism of James's work is without controversy: debates like the one surrounding the governess's visions in "The Turn of the Screw" have raged for years, and show no sign of abating despite recent attempts to shift the critical discourse they depend upon to new and more profitable ground. But this debate, whether intrinsically interesting or not, does nothing to challenge our basic assumptions about James. "Glasses," on the other hand, does—not by an assault from without, but by an invidious undercutting from within. The tracing of the tensions produced thereby will constitute the task of this chapter.

I

A little idea occurred to me the other day for a little tale that *Maupassant would have called* Les Lunettes, *though I'm afraid that* The Spectacles *won't do.*

James, *The Complete Notebooks*

This sentence was entered in James's Notebooks on June 26, 1895, and begins a long outline of the story he proposed to write. Tintner has suggested that James's rejection of "The Spectacles" as a title for his story was a recognition of its previous use by Poe, but it seems clear that Maupassant, not Poe, was on James's mind at the time. Though taken aback by Maupassant's sexual exploits, Henry James remained more than favorably impressed with his fiction, devoting one of his finest critical essays to it, and reminding himself occasionally in the Notebooks to aim for the Maupassant "spirit." But if "Glasses" reminds us, in its surprise ending, of a story like "The Necklace," it must also be admitted that the sentence quoted above specifically *rejects* Maupassant in the matter of titling: "The Spectacles" is spoken of as a translation of "Les Lunettes," and neither is suitable as a title for this particular story. The title finally chosen is "Glasses," not "The Glasses," as Wayne Booth would have it,[2] and what is maintained in that quiet distinction is the denial of the specificity of the definite article.

There are many glasses in "Glasses." Even the most casual reader is struck by James's use of every available synonym for glasses, going so far as to make up a few of his own: eyeglasses, spectacles, specs, pince-nez, nippers, goggles, optic rings, vitreous badge, and so forth. And there are other types of glasses here as well. The narrator remarks that it would have been as impossible to be impertinent to Flora "as it would have been to throw a stone at a plate-glass window."[3] In the climactic scene at the opera, the vibrant Flora is "the aim of fifty tentative glasses" (*GL,* 363). And elsewhere Flora boasts of the many passing strangers magnetized by her glorious face, who, "to gaze their fill at her, had found excuses to thrust their petrifaction through the very glasses of four-wheelers" (*GL,* 332). The effect of this proliferation of glass is manifold in that while emphasizing the dreaded object—Flora's glasses—it also serves notice to the reader that "glasses" is a supercharged term, a kind of nefarious sliding signifier whose each permutation directs the narrative flow while remaining essentially indefinite.

This swirling multiplicity of glasses comes to rest, tentatively, upon the florid face of Mrs. Meldrum. As the narrator's goad and confidante, she provides him, and the reader, with a convenient narrative device—an apparently unimpeachable and reasonably detached source of information regarding Flora and her plight, delivered in the voice of plain common sense. She is "the heartiest, the keenest, the ugliest of women," with "the tread of a grenadier and the voice of an angel," full of "loud sounds and free gestures" (*GL,* 318), and in contrast to the blind spots of the narrator, she offers an invitation to the reader to place his trust in her straightforward view of things. But this may well be a mistake, as the case of Mrs. Meldrum is by no means uncomplicated. In "The Myopic Narrator in Henry James's 'Glasses,'" Sharon Dean points out that there is a persistent tendency for readers of this story to look on Mrs. Meldrum as *old*—older, at least, than the other three characters—a conclusion which is unsupported by a close reading of the text.[4] As Dean convincingly demonstrates, Mrs. Meldrum may be no older than her friends; she may well be Flora's competition for the affections of Geoffrey Dawling. If this is the case, what then is the source of such a compelling misapprehension? There is a variety of textual points one could refer to—Mrs. Meldrum is a widow, the friend of the narrator's mother; she eventually becomes Flora's "guardian"; James speaks of her "motherly hand" upon Dawling's arm (*GL,* 352), and so forth. Each of these points, however, is in the nature of a justification after the fact, aimed at excusing a mistake already made. I would contend, rather, that the viewing of Mrs. Meldrum as old is not a mistake as such, but a selection of one of two seemingly contradictory possibilities that are both palpably there in the text and, in fact, the selection which is most consonant with a satisfying "resolution" of the story. For the problem of Mrs. Meldrum's age resides in her role as a wearer of glasses.

For many people, the taking on of a pair of glasses involves a tacit acknowledgment of the passage of time, and of the onset of decay that is aging. There is reason to believe that James was himself preoccupied with the question of aging during the writing of "Glasses." At age 52, already subject to the periodic attacks of gout that were to continue to plague him, James rebounded from the debacle of *Guy Domville* to immerse himself in the short novel of generational conflict that was serialized under the title *The Old Things,* better known today as *The Spoils of Poynton.* And it must be remembered, too, that James's venture into the theater, while certainly an attempt on his part to conquer a different genre and to capture some of the popular acclaim previously denied him, was in large part an attempt to make money—enough money to afford him a comfortable living in his old age. All three hopes were resoundingly dashed, and the disappointment must have been bitter indeed. During this period, which Leon Edel has characterized as a "black abyss,"[5] and with the great novels of his later phase not yet in sight, James returned once more to the character which had granted him his first major success—the *jeune fille.* Yet, unlike the Daisys and Peonies, the Pansys and Violets that populate much of the Jamesian landscape, Flora Saunt is not threatened from without, by a too-wise world that would imperil her innocence. She is instead threatened from within, by the gradual loss of her vision, by the encroachment of the years.

If the putting on of glasses serves as a defense against the passage of time, then it is a defense that is essentially pathetic, for the adoption of these mechanical contrivances paradoxically serves as an annunciation of the very thing they are meant to remedy: in order to combat the *effects* of aging, one must wear an object that itself publicizes the *fact* of aging. Glasses—spectacles—are devices for seeing out, giving a clearer vision of the outer, other world. But they involve an acknowledgment of that other world, of the imperfect quality of seeing, of decay and the passage of time. Thus, spectacles one sees through become "spectacles" others look at, behold; glasses looking out become looking glasses in, mirrored and mirroring back at the wearer.

Flora rejects the glasses, and with them the inevitability of aging, for, despite the passage of several years of narrative time, Flora herself does not age. Instead she undergoes a series of transformations without growing older. The nature of these transformations, and the curious method of their presentation, will be discussed shortly. For now, it will suffice to note the amusing and not altogether surprising fact that Flora is first seen wearing glasses in a toy shop, the place where play and commerce come together, where childhood and adulthood stand in tenuous and intermingled relation, one to the other. Nor is it surprising, after all, that when Flora "brought her face close to Mrs. Meldrum's . . . it was a marvel that objects so dissimilar should express the same general identity" (*GL,* 319). If Flora's refusal to wear the glasses is a refusal to grow old, to lose the childlike qualities of the Jamesian girl, then the one who takes on the glasses, conversely, *must* grow old in them. Hence the mistake regarding Mrs. Meldrum's age, which is not a mistake after all.

Lest the preceding appear to be a kind of critical syllogism, leading to an inevitable conclusion, it should be remembered that its premises are far from certain. There is, as previously noted, sufficiently convincing evidence to see Mrs. Meldrum as a reasonably young woman, with her relation to Geoffrey

Dawling forming a kind of undeveloped dramatic subplot. Further, her curious self-exclusion at the end of the story embodies a like contradiction: it may either be because she loves Dawling too much or because she hates Flora too much; she has helped "author" the story, but in the end refuses to write to the narrator or even to speak of the matter. In "Glasses," with its obviously unreliable narrator, Mrs. Meldrum would seem to provide a base with which the narrative's truth can be grounded, a safe haven from the narrator's uncertain possibilities. But more than anything else, her inherent self-contradictions point to the arbitrary and problematic nature of such a grounding, to the necessity for the reader to choose an option that will provide firmness to a shifting narrative range. If "Glasses" were produced for the stage, the actress playing Mrs. Meldrum would be faced with the impossible task of appearing both young and old, alternately, at each successive moment. The effect is no less than sinister.

While "glasses" resound throughout this text as a kind of multivalent, unhinged presence, Mrs. Meldrum does not wear "glasses": she sports "goggles," "optic circles," " spectacles," "aids to vision." It is all the more curious, then, that it is Mrs. Meldrum who purports to speak the truth of Flora's condition, in a passage distinguished by its oddity. After attempting to convince the narrator that Flora is less than what she appears to be, and before relating the history of her ailment, the oculist's prescription and her childhood trauma, Mrs. Meldrum notes:

> "She has other drawbacks. . . . Those wonderful eyes are good for nothing but to roll about like sugar-balls—which they greatly resemble—in a child's mouth. She can't use them."
>
> "Use them? Why, she does nothing else."
>
> "To make fools of young men, but not to read or write, not to do any sort of work. She never opens a book, and her maid writes her notes. You'll say that those who live in glass houses shouldn't throw stones. Of course I know that if I didn't wear my goggles I shouldn't be good for much." (*GL,* 323–24)

The moment of revelation, of ostensible truth, is inextricably bound together with, and permeated by, tropes. The focus of our gaze—Flora's eyes and glasses—becomes colored, refracted through the lens of metaphor, paronomasia, proverb and euphemism, emerging in the tangled renaming of sugar-balls, glass houses and goggles. Our plain-speaking Mrs. Meldrum is revealed as conversant with, and conversing in, literature.

II

"Glasses" belongs to the period in which James first began the wholesale importation of dramatic devices into his narratives. His Notebook entries around this time, in which he was engaged in writing both this story and *The Spoils of Poynton,* abound in references to the vocabulary of the dramatic arts—scene, scenario, drama, tragedy—as James consciously sought to salvage the lessons learned during his "wasted years" in the theater. In *Henry James: The Treacherous Years,* Leon Edel has traced the course of these fictive explorations, regarding them finally as crucial first steps in the development of the technique characteristic of James's later phase.[6] Paradoxically, though, the employment of dramatic "scenes" in his short fiction, which was to give James the "compression" and brevity he associated with the mastery of form, produced exactly the opposite: both "Glasses" and *The Spoils of Poynton* far exceeded the word limit originally imposed on them, as James lamented that he had "lost sight too much of the necessary smallness, necessary singleness of the subject" (*NB,* 130).

"Glasses" may be seen as one of the important products of this period of experimentation. The narrative technique which Edel terms "systematic scenic alternation,"[7] a familiar Jamesian trademark, is already present here: portions of the narrative given over wholly to dialogue are succeeded by descriptive reminiscences that, in turn, give way to further dialogue. In "Glasses," four scenes in particular need to be singled out. In each of them, the focus of attention is the narrator and Flora; even though other characters may be present on stage, they recede momentarily into the background. Each of these scenes, further, is characterized by the detailed evocation of place: the first occurs on the coast at Folkestone, the second in the toy shop, the third on the down near Mrs. Meldrum's, and the fourth and last at the opera. What is crucial in these scenes is that, despite any action or speech immediately preceding or following, they each contain a moment in which the two characters, the narrator and Flora, are *frozen,* suspended in time. The effect of this freezing is so instantaneous and so subtly wrought that it is easily overlooked—so much so, in fact, that it is more clearly discernible in its effects than perceived in itself. Nonetheless, these moments can be identified, if only as those moments in which the eyes of Flora and the narrator attempt, and fail, to meet.

Immediately following the death of Minny Temple, Henry James writes to his brother William that the image of what she was, her "charm and essential grace," will remain "all locked away, incorruptibly, within the crystal walls of the past."[8] He writes to his mother that "twenty years hence—what a pure eloquent vision she will be . . . a steady unfaltering luminary in the mind": "Her image will preside in my intellect . . . the more I think of her the more perfectly satisfied I am to have her translated from this changing realm of fact to the steady realm of thought. There she may bloom into a beauty more radiant than our dull eyes will avail to contemplate."[9] If Minny Temple served James as the prototype of his oft-repeated evocations of the American girl, her essence suspended within "crystal walls," then Flora Saunt may be seen as the apotheosis, or perhaps the nadir, of her many incarnations, frozen in the narrator's problematic and troubling attempts to encase her in an ever-growing wall of glass.

It might be objected that these instances of Flora's "freezing" are little more than the capture of her pictorial essence by a narrator who is after all a portrait painter, thus relegating them at best to the realm of the merely photographic. This is an oversimplification, however, in that in the last two instances—on the down and at the opera—the narrator himself forms an essential part of the frozen frame. Further, though each of these moments acts as a prod to the narrative flow, it would be a crucial mistake to describe them as epiphanic. The distinguishing characteristic of the epiphany, as employed for example by Joyce, resides in the sudden revelation of a heretofore unrealized truth: the full content of the epiphany is bestowed upon its witness in an instant, fully, leaving that witness in a state of revelatory plenitude that admits of no misgiving or uncertainty. If James anticipated the Joycean epiphany, he also subverts it, in that in "Glasses" the significance of these revelations is not immediately and transparently clear. On the contrary, there is something within the structure of the frozen scene, something *wrong*, that demands on the part of its viewer an exercise of the art of interpretation: rather than answering questions, they pose further questions, further considerations. What comes to the fore, then, is not revelation, but mediated, complicated authorship. For this reason, these frozen scenes might better be termed *tableaux*, in that, since they depend upon their structural link with action that is to follow, they remain controlled by the flavor of the theater.

In each of the four instances, following immediately upon the capture of Flora within the tableau, there occurs a small portion of the narrative—a dialogic interchange, a "sub-scene"—the structure of which is that Flora is subjected to some sort of stimulus which results in an emotional outburst out of all proportion to the ostensible cause. To enumerate: after the first imaging of Flora against the background of the Folkestone sea, the narrator inquires as to the condition of her eyes and is astonished by her blush and tears, having as he confesses "brought on a commotion deeper than any I was prepared for" (*GL*, 327). In the toy shop, the narrator witnesses Lord Iffield's discovery of Flora's eyeglasses and is driven away by the "quite distressing sight" of "this exquisite creature, blushing, glaring, exposed . . . " (*GL*, 340). On the down, following the antic caper of the narrator caught in a case of mistaken identity, Flora's reaction to what would ordinarily be perceived as a gross insult is abnormally and disconcertingly quiet, so much so that the narrator feels "both as if she were watching my nervousness with a sort of sinister irony and as if I were talking to some different, strange person" (*GL*, 355). And at the opera, the innocent gesture of kissing her hand produces in Flora a reaction of fear and shock "that all the privacy in the world couldn't have sufficed to mitigate" (*GL*, 365), a reaction that can only be explained by her blindness. It is in these four instances that the notion of embarrassment comes once again into play, for it is the nature of an embarrassment to be an emotional response generated as the result of an act out of step in some way with the normal course of social expectations. Without a sense of these expectations being violated, there could be no embarrassment. However, each of Flora's aforementioned reactions is so disproportionately skewed from the course of ordinary expectation that the narrator, faced with unavoidable signs of embarrassment, is led to erect a construction of the larger "normal" situation that will plausibly explain the oddness with which he is confronted. All of the characters in "Glasses" are embarrassed at one point or another, and to one extent or another, but Flora's embarrassments make the narrator *interpret*. And this merely reinforces the fact that what the reader is faced with here is a narrative that is in the process of constructing itself, and that there is no reason to believe that that narration is accurate as a description of Flora's feelings, motives, or condition—that it is anything more than a conventionally satisfying fiction. It is against the backdrop of this presentation of the act and art of storytelling that the frozen scene, the tableau, seems so out of place.

While the four tableaux and their accompanying sub-scenes serve as narrative hinges, it must be remembered that they spur the narrator on in a specific direction: the mystery surrounding them leads him to construct an interpretation that will supply a consistent and logical chain of causes. He is after all an artist and as such is fully aware of the power of stylization—it is precisely this that leads to his derogation of Dawling as "the innocent reader for whom the story is 'really true' and the author a negligible quantity," in whose judgment "the rendering was lost in the subject, quite leaving out the element of art" (*GL*, 329–30). Here "Glasses" begins to touch its nearest neighbor, "The Figure in the Carpet," with its "artist" narrator enmeshed in an interpretive quest, linked as they are by their common type of the good-natured sod Geoffrey Dawling/Drayton Deane who accedes to the secret, if uncomprehendingly, through marriage and the ensuing silence. But if the narrator of "Glasses" can chide Dawling for his failure to look past the representational, and pride himself on having "never encountered the great man at whose feet poor Dawling had most submissively sat and who had addressed him his most destructive sniffs" (*GL*, 336), he is nonetheless well acquainted with the figure of the Master, for in his art, whether painting or writing, he aspires to that very quality of mastery. Faced with the task of retrospectively reading the significance of the tableaux, he must as author, and as a kind of reader, intercede, make sense, interpret. However, if his yarns manage only to entangle Dawling, then Dawling's very simplicity would militate against the idea that these performances are in any way "masterly." Our narrator must instead console himself with the reflection that "when one patched things together it was astonishing what ground they covered" (*GL*, 343).

Perhaps one could say here that it is precisely this attempt to make sense of Flora that causes the narrator's recurrent judgment of her as embodying contradictory qualities: she is strikingly beautiful despite her "scrappy little figure" (*GL*, 323); "nothing in her talk ever matched with anything out of it" (*GL*, 331–32); "she was wanting in mystery, but that after all was her secret" (*GL*, 325). The question that faces the narrator is the same one that faces the reader of this tale: how does one find a firm ground for belief? It is not the content of the multiple observations themselves, not a matter of a "realistic" re-presentation of a perceivable fact that troubles us; it is rather that the act of understanding itself imposes the constraints of consistency. Instead of accepting the mis-related nature of what is, the writer/narrator/painter/reader must mold it into a work of art. But our narrator, if an accomplished portrait painter, is only an apprentice writer: he blunders. Like the audience at *Guy Domville,* he is presented with the accomplished dramatic moment and fails to read it properly—in fact makes a mess of the attempt. If the tableaux, as frozen dramatic scenes, are James's unacknowledged attempts to objectify, within a protective coat of glaze, the embarrassment he suffered at the theater, then he has supplied a suitable audience on whom to revenge himself. Of course, this too is problematic: "Glasses" resists interpretation in that it contains its own diffusion of multiple interpretations. The result is a dissatisfying tendency to see only the surface melodrama of a pretty girl going blind, or to exclude the tale from the accepted canon of James's important works as a failed piece by a troubled writer in a transitional stage—both convenient and comfortable pigeonholings of an unruly text.

If the reader of "Glasses" has difficulty in the location of an authoritative base, then that difficulty finds its reflection in the story's plot. The locus of an authority that determines Flora's situation, that constitutes it, is placed in a character who remains forever concealed, offstage. As his Notebook entry shows, James originally intended for the narrator and Flora to meet for the first time at her *oculist's (NB,* 125–26), but this meeting, and indeed any knowledge of who he is or what he has prescribed, is omitted. In a manner prospective of Kafka, the oculist, whose prescription must be followed to the letter, remains stubbornly resistant to approach or appeal: "it's not a thing to be trifled with" (*GL,* 342). Moreover, to the extent that the narrator attempts—albeit incompletely, or stupidly—to appropriate the seat of authority through his writing, he too must absent himself, and conscientiously avoid any contact with clearly defined action. Thus, though he has the power to bring Dawling together with the subject of the portrait he so admires, he neglects to do so. When Dawling pointedly inquires whether Lord Iffield was rough with Flora in the toy shop, the narrator replies "how can I tell what passed between them?" (*GL,* 341), a lie that remains unremarked upon then or later. And, most tellingly, at the most forcefully violent moments of the plot—Flora's retreat into the glasses, and later her blinding—the narrator chooses the moral equivalent of lighting out for the territories: he goes to America to paint. It would seem that, to the extent that the narrator tries to be an "author," he must protect himself. And it is with this mind that we must consider James's manifold meditation on authorship, and the disclaimer that constitutes the first paragraph of "Glasses."

III

James's Notebook entry of August 11, 1895, begins with some reflections on the various entanglements of plot and character in *The Spoils of Poynton,* and continues as follows:

> What I should like to do, God willing, is to thresh out my little remainder, from this point, tabulate and clarify it, state or summarize it in such a way that I can go, very straight and sharp, to my climax, my denouement. What I feel more and more that I must arrive at, with these things, is the adequate and regular practice of some such economy of clear summarization as will *give* me from point to point, each of my steps, stages, tints, shades, every main joint and hinge, in its place, of my subject—give me, in a word, my clear order and expressed sequence. I can then *take* from the table, successively, each fitted or fitting piece of my little mosaic. When I ask myself what there may have been to show for my long tribulation, my wasted years and patiences and pangs, of theatrical experiment, the answer, as I have already noted here, comes up as just possibly *this*: what I have gathered from it will perhaps have been exactly some such mastery of fundamental statement—of the art and secret of it, of expression, of the sacred mystery of structure. Oh yes—the weary, woeful time has done something for me, has had in the depths of all its wasted piety and passion, an intense little lesson and direction. What that resultant is I must now actively show.[10]

This passage, with its detailed attention to matters of craft combined with a stern commitment to realize the ambition that motivates it, has come to be widely regarded in the criticism as an exemplary instance of the Master's mastery revealed, as though we are permitted a rare glimpse into the inner workshop of a writer about to embark on the journey of his mature greatness armed with a clear view and a firm resolve. But the Notebook passage, examined closely, simply will not bear the weight of such a wishful reading.

First, we are struck by the repeated appearance of an overtly dramatic tone, in both the technical and casual senses of that word. The prolonged lamentations of "my wasted years and patiences and pangs" and "the weary, woeful time," combined with the concluding exhortation to action, come to form what can only be seen as a kind of abortive soliloquy: the reader has been witness to a performance, and may well feel the impulse to applaud. This quality seems doubly strange given the place of its appearance—why would a private notebook contain a passage so obviously meant to be read? It is of little avail to reply that James's Notebooks occasionally contain other passages of a like character. What is important to note is that this passage, instead of taking the usual form of jotted reminders, is composed, constructed with an eye to the effect it will produce in what now must be regarded as a postulated reader. Instead of a moment of covert spying on the secret thoughts of an author, the reader of the Notebook must contend instead with a treatise on authorship that is itself plainly authored: apparently true revelation is deflected through the devices of the fictionalist.

The persistent dramatic tone only highlights the passage's underlying lack of specificity. In an appeal to an "economy of clear summarization," a desire for the narrative to go "very straight and sharp," it is doubly curious that this aim is to be achieved only by a process described by a multiplicity of verbs—"tabulate and clarify," "state or summarize"—and that the objects of these multiple actions are variously "steps," "stages," "tints," "shades," "joints" and "hinges." The belabored paean to the time spent in "theatrical experiment," while promising the revelation of an "intense little lesson," delivers only a diffuse range of undefined possibilities, "the art and secret of it," "the sacred mystery of structure." In the tension between firm, definite statement and playful metaphorizing, James has constructed a piece of fiction that demands of its reader an act of interpretive understanding, an attempt to fill the unexplained gaps with definitions—an effect which an appeal to the justly famed Jamesian circumlocution will in no wise mitigate.

Can it be that this investigation of the notion of authorship carries within it its own destruction? That is to say, the controlling feature of the metaphor of the mosaic is that the act of authoring has shifted from an active doing to a passive taking: the process he must "arrive at" will "*give*" to James the pieces he "can then *take* from the table." Realism, for James, had always entailed the idea of his being a "reporter" of life, thus offering a guarantee of the worth of the fictive proposal by an appeal to what's "real." Here, however, it functions as well in allowing the author to skip out, if you will, on the hazardous issue of his own authority: the repeated deflection of the notion of responsibility that accompanies authorship is enacted by a strategic retreat into the passive, despite the manifest commonplace that books do not write themselves.

All of this, of course, would be so much argument in a vacuum were it not for the fact, heretofore unnoticed, that this passage from the Notebooks finds its way directly into "Glasses," forming the remarkable first paragraph of that short story:

> Yes indeed, I say to myself, pen in hand, I can keep hold of the thread and let it lead me back to the first impression. The little story is all there, I can touch it from point to point; for the thread, as I call it, is a row of coloured beads on a string. None of the beads are missing—at least I think they're not: that's exactly what I shall amuse myself with finding out. (*GL*, 317)

Aside from serving notice that this story is to be told in the first person, and providing a sample of the tone of the narrator's voice, this passage is noteworthy for the way in which it is structurally disconnected from the narrative that follows it. Conventional storytelling begins only with the next paragraph, as the narrator tells us: "I had been all summer working hard in town and then had gone down to Folkestone . . . " (*GL*, 317). Even in this brief excerpt we can see the beginnings of characterization, and of the establishment of setting and chronology—but most importantly we witness a shift into the past tense, as opposed to the current musings of the narrator we found in the first paragraph. The result is that, in comparison with what is to come, this first paragraph of "Glasses" takes on the nature of a prefatory note: qualitatively distinct from the subsequent narration, it offers a brief discourse on the impending act of authorship. Paradoxically enough, if the previously quoted extract from James's Notebooks resembles in many ways a piece of fiction, then this passage from "Glasses," in its halting and elliptical quality, is more than reminiscent of a journal entry. By reading the two simultaneously, as it were, we are able to observe the emergence of several correspondences.

James's injunction to proceed "straight and sharp," for example, is echoed here by the narrator in his resolve to "keep hold" of a story that is "all there." Nonetheless, this resolution is immediately abandoned, lost in the haphazard metaphorizing that would seek to inscribe it. The peculiar mix of metaphors employed here—especially the "thread" and the "row of coloured beads on a string"—recalls the similar maneuver of Mrs. Meldrum, and with it the doubtful veracity characterizing her statements. Moreover, this metaphoric slide from thread to string of beads hearkens back to James's own multiple vacillations amongst "steps" and "stages," "joints" and "hinges," in his orotund descriptions of the procedures of his craft. For both James and the narrator, the relative imprecision of description afforded by this metaphoric flux serves to function not only as a pleasing circumlocution round a difficult subject, but also as a cunning evasion of the mastery seemingly necessary for the rendering of a definitive statement. The thread which our narrator clutches will indeed serve as an Ariadne thread, guiding him through his story, but he nonetheless eludes the heroism of one who would risk the perils of the labyrinth. As James depends upon the mosaic, with each piece "fitted or fitting," to provide him with his "expressed sequence," so too the narrator of "Glasses" relies upon another ornamental artifact, the "row of coloured beads on a string," to furnish him with a structure for his story. Though the metaphors have shifted, the method of composition is the same: an active *controlling* of the disparate portions of the narrative, which one might well expect of an "author," gives way instead to a passive *reception* of a form already constructed in some unspecified elsewhere.

Tracing the first paragraph of "Glasses" from beginning to end, we can see the ultimate effect of this slippage in narrative authority. The staunchly certain affirmations of the narrator—"Yes indeed . . . I can keep hold"—are filtered through the distortions of metaphor only to emerge finally as a doubt, as he grows unsure whether one of the "beads" comprising his little story is missing or not. The resolution of his doubt will ostensibly be achieved through the process of discovery that is the writing of his tale; yet even here the narrator's comment is equivocal, in his shifting of focus from the active venture of "finding out" to the *amusement* that act will afford him. And it is this concluding reference to amusement that is especially telling—first in the implications of what sort of amusement might be garnered from such an apparently woeful tale, and more importantly in the realization that the crucial word "amuse" is itself punningly hinged on the doubled senses of the "muse" of writing and the "amusement" of play. At the moment the author begins to write, as he sits "pen in hand" and surveys the ground before him, he pledges to his readers a lack of seriousness that is the very antithesis of control, an abdication of the authority which is the true province of the Master.

IV

Of course, a comparison of a passage from Henry James's Notebooks with a passage from one of his fictions cannot amount to a virtual translation. The apparent randomness of construction found in the first paragraph of "Glasses" would alone preclude such an exacting reading. Still, even that randomness seems peculiarly appropriate. If the task of "mastery" involves an attempt to make coherent all the otherwise disconnected and separated threads of experience, then a figural portion of a text that would explode the notion of mastery from within must necessarily be something less than coherent. It might perhaps be likened to a row of colored beads on a string: each bead related to every other through resemblance and connection, but discretely separate as well. Or is the string of beads more like a rosary, the implement of prayer? A passage of time in undirected, purposeless repetition, counting off entreaties to an Author who grants existence, truth, certainty—but who does not reply.

One final question remains: could we possibly say that, despite her blindness, Flora Saunt leaves us supremely, gloriously happy? She has, after all, gained everything she hoped for, at a price that, while perhaps too high for most, may never have meant all that much to her. It is a question we cannot answer here, since her blindness thrusts all who know her deep into silence. We shall have to look to James's further rendition of the issues raised in "Glasses," in their reappearance as the central fictive question of "The Liar" and "The Tree of Knowledge."

4

Passing Judgment on "The Liar"

The inclusion of "The Liar" (1888) in a discussion of James's obscure and neglected short fiction would appear at first glance to be somewhat inconsistent. After all, this tale is far from unknown to Jamesian readers: it has occasioned a handful of critical explications, and buttresses the discussion of the "unreliable narrator" found in Wayne Booth's widely regarded *The Rhetoric of Fiction*. One could of course point to the superficial similarities between "The Liar" and "Glasses"—both have a protagonist who is a portrait painter, the silent suffering of Flora Saunt may be forecast in the person of Everina Brant Capadose, and so forth—but this would indeed be an inconsistency, a lapse back into the connection of an obscure text to a better-known, "authorized" one. On the contrary, the linkage between "Glasses" and "The Liar" is far more fundamental, in that despite the quantity of critical attention paid to the latter, this story remains essentially distinct, separated from the established Jamesian canon. It has suffered its share of actual exclusion: even though Oliver Lyon is a portrait painter and no less than five of his works "appear" in the story, "The Liar" failed to find its place in F. O. Matthiessen's edition of James's *Stories of Writers and Artists*.[1] But more importantly, the critical debate surrounding "The Liar" demonstrates a certain profound uneasiness, an inability to locate a satisfactory placement for this story. Not susceptible to charges of triviality, derivation or redundancy, "The Liar" does not suffer its rejection peaceably. It rides the razor's edge between comfortingly authorized masterwork and the unwanted intruder, and that is an uneasy position indeed.

I

Paraphrasing is a distinctly dangerous activity for the literary critic. Any summary he might rehearse runs the risk of slanting the original text toward his preferred reading, so that the very terms he employs become charged with the presuppositions of a contentious reader. This risk is compounded in the case of "The Liar," in that we must come to terms with the sometimes incompatible versions found in the text of the New York Edition versus that of the original book publication—a point I will remark upon later. For now, it suffices to note that what follows in the next paragraph is a summary not of "The Liar" itself—which in a peculiar way resists recuperation through the precis—but of a particular rendering of "The Liar" as it has appeared in the work of several generations of literary critics. We may find that it bears only a tangential relation to the text as constituted by Henry James.

Oliver Lyon, a reasonably young and reasonably successful portrait painter, arrives at a country house in Hertfordshire on commission to paint the venerable old Sir David Ashmore. Amid the glitter of a dinner party, Lyon once again encounters the love of his youth, the beautiful and pure-hearted Everina Brant. Though she had rejected the proposal of marriage made when he was still an art student in Munich, Lyon comes to find that she has accepted instead that of the man seated opposite him at table—the dashingly handsome Colonel Capadose. The adoring glances Everina devotes to her husband serve only to flame Lyon's jealousy—an emotion compounded by the discovery that the Colonel is, in the words of Sir David, a "thumping liar." That the crystalline purity of Everina could acquiesce in such a corrupt union is beyond Lyon's endurance: he becomes obsessed with wringing from her a confession that she would have been happier with him. To this end, Lyon persuades the Colonel to sit for him back in London, and there produces a portrait of the inner nature of this man, a painting entitled simply "The Liar." That Lyon's creation is a masterwork of effect is revealed when he secretly witnesses the couple's reaction to it: Everina's wailing sobs, her horrified shock of recognition are matched by the Colonel's fury as he, with a cry of "damn him, damn him," seizes a dagger and hacks the canvas to pieces. Lyon's victory is completed later when, on confronting the couple, the Colonel exculpates himself through the expected fabrication, and his wife, though gently and obliquely, backs up his story. Lyon exits profoundly shaken by his realization that Everina is content in her possession of "the original." Unable to comprehend the depth of her devotion to her husband, he can only lay the blame upon the Colonel: "he had trained her too well."[2]

If the preceding summary seems tinged with the melodramatic, then its writer has achieved his intended effect. For it was meant to reflect the tacit assumptions of the criticism of "The Liar," a criticism that verges on the melodramatic to the extent that it relentlessly pursues the key figure of a melodrama—the villain. Critical interpretations of "The Liar" seem obsessed with the identification and subsequent castigation of "evil" in this story: convinced that it must be read as a kind of moral fable, they are intent on describing the moral dilemma involved, with an eye toward providing the correct solution to that dilemma, the "true" assignment of culpability in accord with James's real intentions.[3] One school of thought holds that the blame ought to lie most heavily upon Everina: in a reading largely in accord with Lyon's own, these critics feel that "her life, no less than her husband's, is a lie."[4] The final scene of this story supplies the proof that, since she "*does* support her husband's mythomania"[5] in her "cynical" acquiescence in his lie,[6] "her moral being has been altered beyond redemption, her honor corrupted by love."[7] For these critics, Lyon escapes for the most part the stigma of culpability, since, as artist, he "is inspired by the Muse of Truth,"[8] and "the position of the dedicated artist seems at the end far more admirable than that of the loyal wife."[9] Another group of critics, however, would reverse this hierarchy entirely. For them, Everina's complicity in the Colonel's final lie is excused on the grounds of her superior perception and devotion; the focus of judgment shifts instead to Lyon, in that it is his "flaw of jealousy . . . that works the evil in the story."[10] For these critics, "Oliver Lyon is on the point of committing that crime which for both Hawthorne and James was the worst possible: of violating the integrity of another man's personality";[11] he commits what was for James "the chief sin" in his "inhuman and dehumanizing *use* of people."[12] An appeal to the sanctity of Art is to no avail, since in his machinations against the Capadoses he "ceases to function as an artist"[13] and "becomes a vicious agent in the story."[14] The portrait of the Colonel is revealed to be not a true reflection of its model's inner nature but a "masterpiece of treachery" that reveals instead "the progressive degeneration and self-corruption of a rejected and malicious leech."[15]

It should be apparent by now that "The Liar" has engendered a lively critical dispute, but like many protracted arguments, this one can be seen finally to rest upon largely mistaken premises. Even a cursory examination of the tenor of the remarks quoted above will reveal a thoroughgoing and ultimately determinative moralistic bias: "flaw," "sin," "crime," "evil," "vicious," "degeneration," "corruption"—this is the language of judgment, the rendering of a verdict from on high. In their unspoken assumption that, in the words of West and Stallman, "the problem in James's comedy is a moral problem,"[16] critics of "The Liar" have unwittingly restricted themselves to a critical discourse that is inherently limited in its possibilities. In recurrently seeking to decide who is "good" and who is "bad," who is "right" and who is "wrong," one remains forever confined to a set of explanatory categories that are by definition absolutely defined and closed off, and absolutely exclusive of one another. Thus, the debate about "The Liar" is subverted by its own philosophical underpinnings: slavish adherence to the dictates of the "moral" question can only produce critical responses that are always already built into the discourse that enacts them, and the structure of any analysis predicated thereon can only remain subservient to those hidden presuppositions.

Several critics have sought a provisional escape from this viciousness circle in an appeal to the notion of "ambiguity." Much has been made of Jamesian ambiguity, and while this concept has had its usefulness in the exploration of certain Jamesian peculiarities, it would seem that it can also act as a screen for other, less obvious maneuvers, both on James's part and on ours. It has even been suggested that "ambiguity" in the Jamesian text is assigned quite the opposite function from that which it has traditionally been seen to fulfill: Mark Seltzer, for one, has contended that "the 'aesthetic' production of ironies, tensions, and ambiguities in the Jamesian text ultimately serves the authority and interests that these signs of 'literariness' have generally been seen to question or even to subvert."[17] But while this may be true of the canonical James, the James that is available for commentary, what is to be said of those excluded texts that offer, for instance, the ironization of ambiguity, as in "The Liar"? Once again, we see the restrictive operation of exclusion provided by the function of the "author," as guaranteeing and producing a consistency and identity of *oeuvre*, in a striking illustration of what Foucault has described as the author's role as "the unifying principle in a particular group of writings or statements, lying at the origins of their significance, as the seat of their coherence."[18] This power is so strong that it displaces the probe of the critic who is going past one level of systematic misreading, only to find another.

The invocation of ambiguity in the case of "The Liar," then, in order to resolve the critical point of contention regarding "morality" outlined above, amounts to little more than an evasion, an extraordinary case of having one's cake and eating it too. Here, the application of ambiguity involves its displacement from the descriptive to the prescriptive realm, so that one is ultimately able to conveniently avoid any apparent discrepancy that critical investigation might reveal.[19] The resultant effect is simply that of preclusion, a cutting off of the question in a retreat to the undecidable that lacks even the redeeming playfulness of the paradox. Most of all, the appeal to ambiguity, in responding to the question "either/or" with the answer "both," neglects to examine the structure of the original question itself, and refuses to consider whether that question was valid in the first place, or even worth the asking.

One critic deserves special mention in this regard. Ora Segal, in *"The Liar:* A Lesson in Devotion,"[20] provides a reading of "The Liar" that is singularly sensitive to the nuances and complexities of that text, and anticipates what I regard as a necessary relation of "The Liar" to "The Tree of Knowledge." But Segal's resolution of the problems involved in "The Liar" by a recourse to the overwhelming power of "love" must be regarded finally as something less than successful. To turn from the enormously rigid categories of good versus evil toward the healing balm of redemptive love is merely to sink back into the biggest and darkest explanatory category of all, the kingdom of tautology, where all "lies" are resolved by forgiving them, where all contradictions are resolved by disallowing them. Neither Segal nor the readers of ambiguity have managed to escape the fundamental structure of the "moral" argument, which continues to serve as the basis on which all their further complexities rest.

This argument is one of a number of views of this story that are further undermined by a reliance on the New York Edition version of "The Liar," and it is here that some remarks need be made concerning that august edifice in the

Jamesian canon. In the preparation of his works for their collection in the New York Edition, James made a number of minor stylistic revisions, but at times these changes are of such scope as to cause substantive alteration of the texts. Such is the case with "The Liar." Wayne Booth contends that these changes support his view that James ultimately intended to minimize the ambiguities found in "The Liar," and to redirect the reader's attention to the failure of vision which characterizes Oliver Lyon. This is a debatable conclusion, of course, but at least Booth openly recognizes the existence of two competing versions. Most critics of the story, on the other hand, do not, and to the extent that their arguments depend upon the close reading of passages not found in the original, those arguments become suspect. Increasingly, James scholars have come to recognize that the New York Edition —with its extraordinary prefaces, frontispiece photographs and textual changes—must be regarded as occupying a singular place in the corpus of James's works, with an exceedingly complex intertextual relation even to the separate works captured within it. Recent treatments of the Prefaces alone demonstrate that with a text that is part treatise, part memoir and part novel, one must not remain complacent in the view that the New York Edition provides critical truth. In my view, the New York Edition problematizes the reading of Henry James to a remarkable extent, embodying as it does the reflection of Henry James knowingly playing with the image of the Master selecting his own masterpieces, and then only at the distance of some 20 or 30 years and hundreds of narrative miles. I have instead employed throughout this study the versions of the tales as they appeared in their original book publication, and as are conveniently found there or in Leon Edel's edition of *The Collected Tales of Henry James*.[21] To the extent that they consequently avoid one further turn of the screw of mastery, so much the better.

Regardless of which text is employed, however, one result of an unquestioning dependence on the assignment of moral rectitude in this story is a curious and persistent blindness on the part of the critics: it is astonishing to note the commonality of their reference to certain selected portions of this text, to the unanimous neglect of others. It is as though only a fraction of "The Liar" has somehow been predetermined as salient; the rest is ignored. In their attempts to submit the contrariness of this tale to the systematized standards of moral judgment, the critics have relied heavily on one of the characteristic strategies for the perpetuation of mastery: the exclusion of the outlaw. What I propose to do in the next portion of this chapter is to trace the outlines of some of these outlaws, to provide perhaps a more balanced reading of the text as it is actually constituted. We may well find that what the critics have relinquished, in their willingness to read "The Liar" through the grid of morality, is precisely their ability to question whether the text as extant challenges that very submission to systematized principle, to the sovereign hand of authority.

II

As is so often the case in the Jamesian short story, the first paragraph of "The Liar" serves to provide a context, an erection of the borders enclosing the narrative space:

> The train was half an hour late and the drive from the station longer than he had supposed, so that when he reached the house its inmates had dispersed to dress for dinner and he was conducted straight to his room. The curtains were drawn in this asylum, the candles were lighted, the fire was bright, and when the servant had quickly put out his clothes the comfortable little place became suggestive—seemed to promise a pleasant house, a various party, talks, acquaintances, affinities, to say nothing of very good cheer. (*LI*, 383)

The richly evocative description here is characteristically Jamesian, but it carries within it the seed of a metaphor that will prove determinative. The country house at Stayes, seen as an "asylum" complete with "inmates," functions as a brilliant but essentially neutral backdrop, a safe refuge whose stability throws into relief the narrative action that is to follow. That action consists largely of the detailed portraiture of the consciousness that is Oliver Lyon. Even here, the quiet bedroom, with its miscellaneous collection of books and prints, provokes in him various reflections on the nature of his hosts, reflections that reveal to the reader much about Lyon himself—his casually dismissive air of social snobbery, his cleverness and arid wit. But it would be a mistake to think that the fictional exposition of Lyon ceases when he leaves his room, that he becomes a passive observer, a "lucid reflector," of his fellow inmates.

Oliver Lyon is first and foremost an artist, a painter of portraits. His success in his field even entitles him to look upon himself as "something of a celebrity" (*LI*, 384). We will come to see the extent to which Lyon the artist aspires to the position of the Master, his desire to take his place, next to Moroni, among those painters who have produced the "supreme," the "immortal" (*LI*, 420). For the time being, it is important to recognize that Lyon's obsessive pursuit of the perfectly realized image does not come as the result of a bitterly jealous desire for revenge, but is discernibly present in him from the first. Even as Lyon seats himself at table, James makes us privy to his particular philosophy of art:

> When he was working well he found himself in that happy state—the happiest of all for an artist—in which things in general contribute to the particular idea and fall in with it, help it on and justify it, so that he feels for the hour as if nothing in the world can happen to him, even if it come in the guise of disaster or suffering, that will not be an enhancement of his subject. (*LI*, 384)

What is crucial here is the notion that, for Lyon, all is for the best when "things in general contribute to the particular idea." This passion for *consistency,* for the conjunction of the separate threads of experience into a logically unified whole, will come to form Lyon's special burden, and will ultimately serve as the necessary basis of all subsequent complications of the narrative.

The first telling instance of Lyon-as-logician occurs as he turns his attention to his neighbors at dinner. During a lull in the conversation, "so that he had time to lose himself in his favourite diversion of watching face after face" (*LI*, 386), Lyon makes the following observations, most profitably viewed all together:

> His neighbour had a sociable manner and evidently was accustomed to quick transitions; she turned from her other interlocutor with a methodical air, as a good cook lifts the cover of the next sauce-pan. (*LI*, 387)

> The gentleman on his left at last risked an observation, and they had some fragmentary talk. This personage played his part with difficulty: he uttered a remark as a lady fires a pistol, looking the other way. (*LI*, 388)

> She was a large, bright, negative woman, who had the same air as her husband of being somehow tremendously new; a sort of appearance of fresh varnish (Lyon could scarcely tell whether it came from her complexion or from her clothes), so that one felt she ought to sit in a gilt frame, suggesting reference to a catalogue or a price-list. (*LI*, 385)

> Even if Arthur Ashmore would not be inspiring to paint . . . even if he had looked a little less like a page (fine as to print and margin) without punctuation, he would still be a refreshing, iridescent surface. (*LI*, 386)

These brief characterizations, of his immediate neighbors to right and left and Mrs. and Mr. Ashmore, respectively, are themselves united by a single thread. What must certainly stand out for the reader is not so much the content of the metaphors themselves as the deftness of their execution. James J. Kirschke has noted that James "drew upon his knowledge of Impressionism for his splendid characterizations of the dinner party guests," but that, "as with many Impressionist works of art, the reader here must supply the missing elements, must imagine for himself how James's characters look."[22] I would contend, on the contrary, that it is the nature of these descriptions not to invite further supplementation, but to *preclude* it. In each case, James has rendered Lyon's perception of his fellow diners in a metaphor so strikingly original and precise that it has the effect of capturing its object in an image no less perfectly realized than one of Lyon's portraits. In a reversal of metaphor's usual expansiveness, these "masterful" descriptions close off the discussion of their referents, in an act of categorization that leads quickly to dismissal—the essence of cleverness.

As Lyon broadens his gaze from the relatively trivial individual diners to the larger and more important composition of the group, we are given this remarkable passage:

> Oliver Lyon took but a few steps into the wide saloon; he stood there a moment looking at the bright composition of the lamplit group of fair women, the single figures, the great setting of white and gold, the panels of old damask, in the centre of each of which was a single celebrated picture. There was a subdued lustre in the scene and an air as of the shining trains of dresses tumbled over the carpet. At the furthest end of the room sat Mrs Capadose, rather isolated; she was on a small sofa, with an empty place beside her. Lyon could not flatter himself she had been keeping it for him; her failure to respond to his recognition at table contradicted that, but he felt an extreme desire to go and occupy it. Moreover he had her husband's sanction; so he crossed the room, stepping over the tails of gowns, and stood before his old friend. (*LI*, 396)

The celebrated portraitist must not restrict his concern to the central subject of his creation, but must also pay close attention to the subtle shadings of background, the overall sense of *composition*. That Lyon the painter appreciates compositional values is hardly surprising, but the crux of the passage quoted above lies not merely in this appreciation, but in his fastening on to the gap in the fabric of that composition. Lyon's compulsion to fill the empty space beside Everina Capadose is as much the result of his obsession with a sense of wholeness, with the perfectly realized and perfectly completed canvas, as it is of his desire to renew his proximity to an erstwhile lover.

As Everina Capadose enters the narrative frame, we need to turn our attention briefly to Lyon's special perception of her. The portions of this text where Lyon's idealized conception of her pristine innocence is stated and restated are too numerous and evident to bear repetition. She is the perfectly simple, perfectly desirable object onto which he projects his regularized, biweekly fantasies. What does deserve special mention is the way in which Lyon deals with a perceived threat to the integrity of that conception. When Mrs. Capadose confesses the sale of Lyon's painting, we are witness to this conversation:

> "When you come to see me in London (I count on your doing that very soon) I shall see you looking all round. I can't tell you I keep it in my own room because I love it so, for the simple reason——" And she paused a moment.
> "Because you can't tell wicked lies," said Lyon.
> "No, I can't. So before you ask for it——"
> "Oh, I know you parted with it—the blow has already fallen," Lyon interrupted. (*LI*, 398)

Note here the way in which the ellipses in Everina's explanation are promptly filled by Lyon, and in a way that is consonant with his idealization of her. It is manifestly clear that the reason she can't say she keeps it in her room is that she no longer keeps it anywhere, but Lyon's rush to supplement her pause deflects that confession, and in a way that turns it back into a further confirmation of what for him is an immutable truth.

Further, when his image of her undergoes a real and potentially decisive threat, from the revelation provided by Sir David that not only is the Colonel a liar but that his wife has backed him up in his lies, Lyon embarks on a series of reflections on "what the loyalty of a wife and the infection of an example would have made of an absolutely truthful mind":

> Did she sit in torment while her husband turned his somersaults, or was she now too so perverse that she thought it a fine thing to be striking at the expense of one's honour? It would have taken a wondrous alchemy—working backwards, as it were—to produce this latter result. Besides these two alternatives (that she suffered tortures in silence and that she was so much in love that her husband's humiliating idiosyncrasy seemed to her only an added richness—a proof of life and talent), there was still the possibility that she had not found him out, that she took his false pieces at his own valuation. A little reflection rendered this hypothesis untenable; it was too evident that the account he gave of things must repeatedly have contradicted her own knowledge. Within an hour or two of his meeting them Lyon had seen her confronted with that perfectly gratuitous invention about the profit they had made off his early picture. Even then indeed she had not, so far as he could see, smarted, and—but for the present he could only contemplate the case. (*LI*, 408–9)

I have taken the liberty of quoting this passage at such length because the sheer weight of its machinery must be fully seen to be fully appreciated. Long passages of introspection are no stranger to James's work—one thinks immediately of Isabel Archer, John Marcher, especially Maggie Verver—but the musings of Oliver Lyon have been restricted, by James, to reflect the painter's most salient characteristic. Emptied of their specific content, the statements in this passage reveal the Aristotelian linearity of a persistently logical mind. Hypotheses are advanced and discarded, evidence is sifted and weighed, alternatives explored and conclusions proved, all in the effort to rationally deduce a solution to a postulated problem. Faced with a formidable assault by the unconscionable, the inconceivable, the superrational Lyon responds with his most incisive logic, wielded now as a defensive weapon in an effort to guard the sanctity of his tiny, private temple.

But if Lyon's logic is incisive, it is by no means decisive. What we are faced with in "The Liar," the fulcrum of this narrative's action, is the increasing inability of Lyon's logic to effectively squelch the contradictions that assail it: the passionate consistency that is his hallmark becomes more and more unable to assimilate a series of challenges that are predominately extra-rational and relentlessly inconsistent. Even as Lyon patronizingly stamps Arthur Ashmore as a "refreshing, iridescent surface," his attention is arrested: "But the gentleman four persons off—what was he? Would he be a subject, or was his face only the legible door-plate of his identity, burnished with punctual washing and shaving—the least thing that was decent that you would know him by?" (*LI*, 386). That gentleman is, of course, Colonel Capadose. But while the metaphoric encapsulations of the other diners, as noted above, shine in their glib and crystalline brilliance, the snaring of the Colonel is not so simple. The metaphor of the door-plate seems only marginally successful by comparison, and its effect is further confounded by the oblique and ominously troubling reference to decency that concludes it. What is most important to note here, however, is that the rendition of this metaphor, rather than taking the form of a definite statement, appears instead in the alternative grammatical form of the *question*. The deft dismissal of the categorizer is replaced by a troubled inquiry—what is he?

Lyon, however, is not easily put off, and the very next paragraph houses his further attempt at a quick verbal sketch of the Colonel:

> This face arrested Oliver Lyon: it struck him at first as very handsome. The gentleman might still be called young, and his features were regular: he had a plentiful, fair mustache that curled up at the ends, a brilliant, gallant, almost adventurous air, and a big shining breastpin in the middle of his shirt. He appeared a fine satisfied soul, and Lyon perceived that wherever he rested his friendly eye there fell an influence as pleasant as the September sun—as if he could make grapes and pears or even human affection ripen by looking at them. What was odd in him was a certain mixture of the correct and the extravagant: as if he were an adventurer imitating a gentleman with rare perfection or a gentleman who had taken a fancy to go about with hidden arms. He might have been a dethroned prince or the war-correspondent of a newspaper: he represented both enterprise and tradition, good manners and bad taste. Lyon at length fell into conversation with the lady beside him—they dispensed, as he had had to dispense at dinner-parties before, with an introduction—by asking who this personage might be. (*LI*, 386–87)

At first the description is wholly conventional—the Colonel is young and handsome, his mustache and breastpin draw comment, and so forth. But conventionality soon gives way as we begin to focus on what is "odd" in him. What emerges then is a series of alternative suggestions, four pairs of polar opposites: gentleman vs. adventurer, dethroned prince vs. war-correspondent, enterprise vs. tradition, good manners vs. bad taste. It is strikingly appropriate that we finally spin back to the fundamental and categorical opposition of conventional morality—good vs. bad—since it is precisely Lyon's dependence on such a reductive ethical scheme that is powerless to come to grips with the Colonel. Colonel Capadose stands astride Lyon's predetermined categories and eludes, for the moment, Lyon's attempts to encapsulate him, embodying as he does the "odd" collusion of mutually exclusive qualities. The result is that Lyon is sent scrambling back for more information, more answers to more questions—the typical maneuver of the puzzled logician.

When Lyon finds himself unable to neatly resolve the contradictions in the Colonel's appearance, he turns instead to his wondrous productions. Though Capadose may be at first the "liar platonic," Lyon is finally convinced that his lies are capable of malicious effect—a point that is "proven" with the Colonel's pinning the blame for the destruction of his portrait on the innocent Geraldine. Those critics who would take Lyon's view of things have generally agreed with him that the Colonel's treatment of this woman offers conclusive evidence of his moral deficiency, while those who take a more kindly view toward the Capadoses counter that it is far better to accuse an unknown woman who will never be heard from again than to rip away the social facade which hides the real truth of their crime. Neither argument seems very convincing, for the simple reason that the critics of morality fail to regard this mysterious woman with sufficient attention.

Geraldine/Grenadine enters the story in a manner so abrupt that it is as though she had dropped from the sky. Her employment by James could of course be read as a particularly crude instance of authorial intervention, where a character who has no other intrinsic connection to the plot is introduced only to provide a convenient device for the resolution of that plot. I would argue, however, that this character is in a sense even more "undeveloped" than that. Here, James takes an only partially molded lump of fictive clay, and hands it to his two surrogate authors—Lyon and Capadose—to see what they will do with it. What the Colonel does with it is readily remembered by readers of this story, but the work of Lyon in this respect is often overlooked. Upon her entrance, as she stands silently before the two men, Lyon notices her first and responds thus: "'Oh, dear, here's another!' Lyon exclaimed, as soon as his eyes rested on her. She belonged, in fact, to a somewhat importunate class—the model in search of employment" (*LI*, 422). His judgment is instantaneous, and one, you'll note, of *classification*, such that the figure before him is immediately subjected to a predetermined category that serves to fully determine her status. From this act of reductive pigeonholing it is only a short step to dismissal: after a question to establish her means of entry, "Lyon went on with his painting; he had given her a sharp look at first, but now his eyes lighted on her no more. The Colonel, however, examined her with interest" (*LI*, 422). Lyon's construction of the Geraldine-fiction is soon finished, her possibilities exhausted. It is enough for him to notice that "she was rather soiled and tarnished, and after she had been in the room a few moments the air, or at any rate the nostril, became acquainted with a certain alcoholic waft" (*LI*, 422), in order to have done with her. It is not surprising, finally, that one who is for Lyon little more than a boozy whore can be resurrected later as the "innocent" victim of the Colonel's lies, for what would seem to be a vacillation on Lyon's part is eminently consistent with a hierarchy of moral law. Alone, the Geraldine-fiction is categorized and dismissed for its intrinsic and obvious "evil," but is easily recuperated as sacrificial lamb in comparison with the greater evil of the Colonel—all without apparent discrepancy, all perfectly consistent with the hierarchy of evil in which Lyon is enslaved.

In contrast, the Colonel's Grenadine-fiction displays the dominant feature of all his lies: it is *productive*. If we leave aside for a moment the question of morality, what we find in the yarn he spins around the model is the exact opposite of Lyon's facile disposal: she is given a history, motives, a desire for revenge—she becomes an individual, even to the necessity of bestowing upon her her own distinctive name. What the Grenadine-fiction does finally is to grant to the nameless model a fund of possibilities, a future. Where Lyon's fiction remains closed off, absolutely determined by the narrow confines of authoritarian discourse, the Colonel's opens out on a limitless potentiality—in that sense it is "productive," for it contains a potential issue.

In retrospect, each of the Colonel's lies can now be seen to possess exactly this quality. Each of them shares the common ambience of the exotic and each is constructed not out of whole cloth, but as an embellishment of the situation with which he is confronted, an embroidery around the edges of the real. But what is crucial to note is how each of his lies contains within it the seed of its own destruction. When the Colonel lies about the disposition of Lyon's painting of Mrs. Capadose, with the story of how they received a "magnificent old vase" in return for it, he tells Lyon that "if you'll come and see us in town she'll show you the vase" (*LI*, 395). With this teasing challenge, Colonel Capadose practically assures that his lie will be uncovered. The clinician might argue that a desire for exposure is a typical adjunct of the pathological liar, but James's exposition of the Colonel's foible is far more interesting than that. When the Colonel pauses to analyze the case of his friend in India who had been buried alive, and the voice that called to him in the night, he observes: "'That's the interesting point. Now *what was it*? It wasn't his ghost, because he wasn't dead. It wasn't himself, because he couldn't. It was something or other! You see India's a strange country—there's an element of the mysterious: the air is full of things you can't explain.'" (*LI*, 394). Here the procedures of the logician are thrown back in Lyon's face, as the Colonel not only bends the truth but laughs at it as well. The objective truth is conquered, assimilated, and comes back as part of the structure of the lie itself. The result is a thing you truly can't "explain."

If the Colonel is viewed as the "liar platonic," what can we now say of his partner in that production, the elusive Mrs. Capadose? At first, Lyon's attempts at her descriptive capture pursue the same structure that he used with the Colonel—the conjunction of opposites: "'And then there's something in her face—a sort of Roman type, in spite of her having such an English eye. In fact, she's English down to the ground; but her complexion, her low forehead and that beautiful close little wave in her dark hair make her look like a glorified *contadina*'" (*LI*, 391). But this strategy rapidly gives way to a more penetrating gaze. Lyon's assertion that "of the most charming head in the world . . . there could never be a replica" (*LI*, 389) is somewhat disingenuous, for he had made repeated attempts to create that replica himself. The one that monopolizes his memory is a sketch of the young Everina Brant as Werther's Charlotte, cutting bread and butter while her little brothers and sisters cluster around her. But we find that this portrait, which Lyon holds so dear, is not after all the one which Everina had kept and later sold. The revelation of Lyon's mistake appears in a conversation between him and the Colonel, and carries with it some extraordinary implications:

"Wasn't there something about a picture? Yes; you painted her portrait."

"Many times," said the artist; "and she may very well have been ashamed of what I made of her."

"Well, I wasn't, my dear sir; it was the sight of that picture, which you were so good as to present to her, that made me first fall in love with her."

"Do you mean that one with the children—cutting bread and butter?"

"Bread and butter? Bless me, no—vine leaves and a leopard skin—a kind of Bacchante."

"Ah, yes," said Lyon; "I remember. It was the first decent portrait I painted. I should be curious to see it to-day." (*LI*, 394–95)

The absent painting is in a sense doubly absent: no longer in the possession of Mrs. Capadose, it has eluded as well the call of Lyon's memory. When it is recovered through the Colonel's reminder, what emerges most forcefully are the conflicting natures of the two representations, the way in which they participate in diametrically opposed categories: Werther vs. Bacchante, the pastoral vs. the bacchanal, the Apollonian vs. the Dionysian. When Lyon and Mrs. Capadose examine precisely this issue of his rendering of her, we find that "Mrs Capadose said before she went away that her husband would probably comply with his invitation, but she added, 'Nothing would induce me to let you pry into *me* that way!' 'Oh, you,' Lyon laughed—'I could do you in the dark!'" (*LI*, 419). Lyon may well be compelled to "do" her in the dark because, to the extent that Everina remains for him the votary of Bacchus, she is one with the dark, apart from the light of the Apollonian day which illuminates all of Lyon's "compositions."

The obvious tinge of sensuality discernible in the passage just quoted remains largely suppressed throughout "The Liar." Robert Gale has pointed out the connection of this story with *The Europeans* through their common reference to what he calls "James's Munchhausenland," the fictional province of Silberstadt-Schreckenstein.[23] While Baroness Eugenia Munster and Colonel Clement Capadose both refer to Silberstadt-Schreckenstein, and both tell lies, the most important connection between these two narratives lies not with the characters just mentioned, but with the resemblance between Oliver Lyon and Robert Acton. Acton, it must be remembered, flees from Eugenia's clutches because "she is not honest, she is not honest . . . she is a woman who will lie."[24] The playful, punning reference to a woman who will "lie" insinuates that Acton's rejection of Eugenia is less the result of a passion for verisimilitude than it is a flight from passion itself, and from an acknowledged sexual initiate. And the similarities between the two persist beyond this: the cool logicality that characterizes Lyon can be ascribed as well to the gentle reasonings of Robert Acton:

From the first she had been personally fascinating; but the fascination now had become intellectual as well. He was constantly pondering her words and motions; they were as interesting as the factors in an algebraic problem. This is saying a good deal; for Acton was extremely fond of mathematics. . . . It was part of his curiosity to know why the deuce so susceptible a man was *not* in love with so charming a woman. If her various graces were, as I have said, the factors in an algebraic problem, the answer to this question was the indispensible unknown quantity. The pursuit of the unknown quantity was extremely absorbing; for the present it taxed all Acton's faculties.[25]

But the comparison of Lyon to Acton goes only so far. While Acton manages to elude the deceitful Baroness, largely through his passivity, Lyon remains fascinated by the strange impenetrability, the otherness, of Everina Brant Capadose. She is for him like "some fine creature from an asylum—a surprising deaf-mute or one of the operative blind" (*LI*, 396). The image of the asylum that began the story returns here in full force, but reversed. While an asylum is a refuge, a place of sanctuary set apart from its surroundings, its inmates are by definition "misfits"—those who would refuse to conform to established rules, and who are therefore separated from the rest by the hand of authority that imposes those standards. Yet, curiously enough, the misfit is thereby only emphasized— the isolation which defines the asylum serves only to fortify his otherness.

At those moments when Lyon directly confronts that which is elemental in Mrs. Capadose, a remarkable phenomenon occurs in the text of this story. Consider: "There was nothing between them to-day and he had no rights, but she must have known he was coming (it was of course not such a tremendous event, but she could not have been staying in the house without hearing of it), and it was not natural that that should absolutely fail to affect her" (*LI*, 389). In contrast to the uniformity of Lyon's other introspections, the rhetorical form of the remarks quoted above demonstrates a subtle yet crucial alteration. In place of the rational and logical tone of Lyon's musings, the firm declarative statements to which we have become accustomed, James here substitutes a series of sentences distinguished most notably by their negativity. "They were a remarkable couple, Lyon thought, and as he looked at the Colonel standing in bright erectness before the chimney-piece while he emitted great smoke-puffs he did not wonder that Everina could not regret she had not married *him*" (*LI*, 400). Note especially the repeated use of the "not" in the statements at hand. The employment of multiple negatives is admittedly a Jamesian signature, but here they function as a series of indicators, significant in their marking of moments when Lyon the logician cannot "comprehend" Everina the magician.

Oh, he held it as immutably established that whatever other women might be prone to do she, of old, had been perfectly incapable of a deviation. Even if she had not been too simple to deceive she would have been too proud; and if she had not had too much conscience she would have had too little eagerness. It was the last thing she would have endured or condoned—the particular thing she would not have forgiven. (*LI*, 408)

As Lyon approaches the mysterious darkness of Mrs. Capadose, her immutable and impenetrable otherness, he is driven away. The discourse that encompasses his thought is inverted, turning from the definite affirmative to an indefinite series of denials, as Everina Capadose resists the mastery inherent in Lyon's categorizations. It is not that she transcends those categories—for "transcendence" would surely form part of Lyon's arsenal—she is just *not in* them.

With the blackness that is Everina squarely before him, Lyon in his frustration addresses himself to her affliction, and his analysis of the lie is most thorough. His conclusion is this: "For a fib told under pressure a convenient place can usually be found, as for a person who presents himself with an author's order at the first night of a play. But the supererogatory lie is the gentleman without a voucher or a ticket who accommodates himself with a stool in the passage" (*LI,* 412). When logic meets its opposite, the rational turns into rationalization. The result is but a metaphor, the mark of the author's authority.

III

I append here some brief remarks about "The Tree of Knowledge" (1900) in view of what seems to me an intimate relation between that story and "The Liar." Both feature a "fraudulent" husband and an adoring, forgiving wife; both present the outsider—Oliver Lyon or Peter Brench—who abhors the husband's productions while desiring his mate. Moreover, "The Tree of Knowledge" shares the same fate as "The Liar" in the neglect and exclusion it has suffered, as James himself recognized when he said of this tale and "The Abasement of the Northmores" that "they were to find nowhere, the unfortunates, hospitality and the reward of their effort" (*AN,* 235). This remark, from the Prefaces, is followed by James's relation of "the grain of suggestion, the tiny air-blown particle" that served as the inspiration for this tale—the story of a young man who discovers the failure of his father's artistic career. But this anecdote, like so many in the Prefaces, is ultimately misleading, for the young Lancelot Mallow is manifestly not the key figure in the story: he serves only as the catalyst for the undoing of Peter Brench.

In a direct reversal of Lyon's attempts to gain a confession from Mrs. Capadose that her husband is a "thumping liar," Peter Brench pursues exactly the opposite goal—it is his task to make sure that Mrs. Mallow never learns that her husband is a "muff" of a sculptor. And it is no easy task, for James's portrait of this "Master" is devastatingly ironic. Morgan Mallow is not only a flop, he is a pretentious flop: "the brown velvet, the becoming *beretto,* the 'plastic' presence, the fine fingers, the beautiful accent in Italian and the old Italian factotum," all these cannot atone for the fact that he possessed "everything of the sculptor but the spirit of Phidias."[26] The description of the Master's creations as seen through Brench's eyes is hilarious:

> The room in which they sat was adorned with sundry specimens of the Master's genius, which had the merit of being, as Mrs Mallow herself frequently suggested, of an unusually convenient size. They were indeed of dimensions not customary in the products of the chisel and had the singularity that, if the objects and features intended to be small looked too large, the objects and features intended to be large looked too small. The Master's intention, whether in respect to this matter or to any other, had, in almost any case, even after years, remained undiscoverable to Peter Brench. The creations that so failed to reveal it stood about on pedestals and brackets, on tables and shelves, a little staring white population, heroic, idyllic, allegoric, mythic, symbolic, in which "scale" had so strayed and lost itself that the public square and the chimney-piece seemed to have changed places, the monumental being all diminutive and the diminutive all monumental; branches, at any rate, markedly, of a family in which stature was rather oddly irrespective of function, age and sex. They formed, like the Mallows themselves, poor Brench's own family—having at least, to such a degree, the note of familiarity. (*TK*, 100)

Brench's efforts to conceal the truth from Mrs. Mallow are not only unsuccessful, they are unnecessary: Lance's Parisian education reveals only that Mrs. Mallow had always known the truth, and the fragile architecture of Brench's concealment crumbles around him.

While Mallow is a caricature of the Master, it is often overlooked that there are in fact two "Masters" in "The Tree of Knowledge." James tells us this of Peter Brench:

> He had "written," it was known, but had never spoken—never spoken, in particular, of that; and he had the air (since, as was believed, he continued to write) of keeping it up in order to have something more—as if he had not, at the worst, enough—to be silent about. Whatever his air, at any rate, Peter's occasional unmentioned prose and verse were quite truly the result of an impulse to maintain the purity of his taste by establishing still more firmly the right relation of fame to feebleness. (*TK*, 94–95)

Brench's artistic impulse, if partially suppressed in the matter of his own creations, finds an outlet in the role of critic: his judgment of Mallow's work noted above, in its invocation of "scale," presumes an authority sufficiently commanding to allow for it. But Brench's fullest expression of the will to mastery takes the form of orchestration: in his manipulation of Lance's career through bribe and extorted promises, Brench resembles the playwright who, hidden in the wings, controls the flow of the drama—until he finds that his actors have abandoned the play. A few years later, another of James's aging gentlemen will discover, like Brench, that the controlling scenario of his life has been predicated on a mistake, and his horror and abasement are of a wholly tragic dimension—I speak, of course, of John Marcher. In 1900, however, James withheld the dignity of the tragic from Peter Brench: his self-delusion is met only with ridicule. The "arch and dewy" Mrs. Mallow, we come to find, has in her deep duplicity not only eluded Brench, she has laughed at his desire. When Brench confides that he had hoped Lance's "passion" for art would "burn out," she makes this response: "'But why should it,' she sweetly smiled, 'with his wonderful heredity? Passion is passion—though of course, indeed, you, dear Peter, know nothing of that. Has the Master's ever burned out?' " (*TK*, 96).

The title of "The Tree of Knowledge" refers, of course, to Brench's desire to keep Lance from Paris, where his learning the truth about the Master might threaten to upset their precarious arrangement. At the same time, "The Tree of Knowledge" must also recall the original voice of interdiction, the command that said thou shalt not partake. Here too, perhaps, we may find the reason for this story's canonical expulsion. To create a failed and silly "Master" like Mallow is tolerable, since by comparison the image of the true Master is left intact. To oppose the Master with a contentious son is likewise allowable, for the dignity therein granted to the object of attack can only serve to strengthen that object. But to create *two* would-be Masters, each no less foolish than his counterpart, and to greet this mirroring only with gentle derision and mockery—this is to explode mastery itself, in subjecting it to the profoundly dangerous threat of humor. Such a transgression cannot be tolerated, even on the part of Henry James the Master. This sweetly charming story, delightfully infused with quiet laughter, could not find a place in a magazine: it first appeared in the collection of short stories appropriately entitled *The Soft Side*.

5

Putting the Screws to the Reader:
"The Third Person"

*The children's innocence is really innocent and their corruption
really corrupt—of this James convinces us by his masterly rendering of both.*
Dorothea Krook, *The Ordeal of Consciousness in Henry James*

Dorothea Krook's pronouncement on "The Turn of the Screw," quoted above,
would seem in fact to encapsulate the interminable critical controversy surrounding that Jamesian standard. The coexistence of opposites—here "innocence" and
"corruption"—circumscribes the often invoked notion of "ambiguity," and the
passion which in turn so often animates the readings of this ambiguity reappears
here within the doubled appeal of "really . . . really"; all, of course, taking place
under the aegis of the Master's hand. When Henry James the Master spoke of "The
Turn of the Screw" as having "the unattackable ease of a perfect homogeneity," of
being of the kind "least apt to be baited by earnest criticism," due to the "conscious
provision of prompt retort to the sharpest question that may be addressed to it," he
could not have anticipated the barrage of questions, critical and otherwise, that has
been leveled at it by its critics (*AN,* 169). In fact, such a torrent of ink has been
loosed on this hapless tale that even the apologies made for spilling just a *few* more
drops have become irritatingly redundant.

No such apology is offered here, nor is one necessary, for the simple reason
that this chapter is addressed *not* to "The Turn of the Screw." My summons of that
tale is not, however, intended as some kind of clever diversion, nor is its dismissal
cavalier. Every serious reader of Henry James returns to his fiction "affected," for
better or worse, and to one extent or another, by the phenomenon that is the most
criticized and perhaps the most famous mainstay of the Jamesian canon. I invite
here the conscious and purposely unspecified recall of that phenomenon, for only
with that recall in hand can we approach "The Turn of the Screw"'s curious and
baffling *Doppelgänger,* the ghostly double entitled "The Third Person." If we

emerge with a clearer view of the former tale, we will have gained much—but that seems most unlikely. As even the governess comes to realize, neither ghostly doubles nor doubled ghosts are by nature submissive.

I

Of all the short stories addressed in this book, "The Third Person" is perhaps the one most richly deserving the label of exclusion. Omitted from the New York Edition, it thus receives no discussion in the Prefaces; nor have James's historians found reference to it in the Notebooks, making it one of only a half dozen or so of his short productions which fail to be mentioned there. The only comment of the Master himself on this tale would seem to be that of his letter to his literary agent J. B. Pinker, whom he directed to reserve the publication of "The Third Person" for *The Soft Side* (1900) since, though written for *The Atlantic Monthly,* James had decided it "would not sell there and was too long to sell elsewhere."[1]

The sparsity of James's comment on this story is but mirrored on the part of his critics. Only two critics, in fact—Leon Edel and Edward Stone—have seen fit to speak of it at any length. Edel, in an introduction to "The Third Person" in his edition of *The Ghostly Tales of Henry James,* draws attention to the similarity between the fictional town of Marr and the actual one of Rye, between the newly acquired home of the Misses Frush and Lamb House.[2] In *Henry James: The Treacherous Years, 1895–1901,* Edel returns briefly to the story, this time offering an embryonic and generally unconvincing reading of "The Third Person" as a fictional reenactment of Henry's sibling rivalry with the then visiting—and ailing—William James. Edward Stone, on the other hand, employs "The Third Person" to make some tentative comments on the relation between James and Hawthorne, especially as regards *The Scarlet Letter.*[3] The common bond between each of these critical commentaries—and their common drawback—is their dependence on matters wholly extratextual. Whether biographical or historical, the substance of all three of these readings consists in the presentation of details for the most part extraneous to the story itself. If, as Edward Stone puts it, "The Third Person" is a "flawless little gem," then it would also seem to possess the characteristic hardness of a gemstone: a resistance to penetration, the scratchings of critical reading.

What can account for this enduring silence? Can it be the only possible critical response to a shimmering, smooth surface? On first inspection, "The Third Person" would appear as a sort of mirrored image of "The Turn of the Screw": one troubled spinster confronted by two ghosts doubles back into one ghost troubled by two confounded spinsters. Each story bears a mystifying confidante—Mrs. Grose vs. Mr. Patten—each has unread letters, each performs a doubled exorcism. If "The Turn of the Screw" has been subject to repeated attempts at penetration, why does "The Third Person" elude a like critical onslaught?

Our first clue resides, perhaps, with the estimable Misses Frush. Joint beneficiaries of their late aunt's will, Susan and Amy Frush take possession of the old house at Marr:

> So it was that they met: Miss Amy accompanied by the office-boy of the local solicitor, presented herself at the door of the house to ask admittance of the caretaker. But when the door opened it offered to sight not the caretaker, but an unexpected, unexpecting lady in a very old waterproof, who held a long-handled eyeglass very much as a child holds a rattle. Miss Susan, already in the field, roaming, prying, meditating in the absence on an errand of the woman in charge, offered herself in this manner as in settled possession; and it was on that idea that, through the eyeglass, the cousins viewed each other with some penetration even before Amy came in. Then at last when Amy did come in it was not, any more than Susan, to go out again.[4]

The decisive image contained in this passage—that of the two Misses Frush staring at each other through a glass—will serve to circumscribe the enduring crisis of identity that these characters enact. Throughout "The Third Person," Susan and Amy Frush will appear as odd duplicates of each other. From their common benighted Victorian virginity to the thoughts they engender in concert, the two Misses Frush seem to be practically interchangeable, two faces of the same indelibly stamped coin.

And yet, at the same time, their apparent identity is often manufactured precisely on the basis of a diametric opposition. Even the triviality of naptime can become figural: "Miss Amy took her evening nap before dinner, an hour at which Miss Susan could never sleep—it was so odd; whereby Miss Susan took hers after that meal, just at the hour when Miss Amy was keenest for talk" (*TP*, 136). This layering of identity and difference together is prefigured in James's initial description of the two, where he notes that Susan, though a lifelong European traveler, "would have served with peculiar propriety as a frontispiece to the natural history of the English old maid," while Miss Amy, "though formed almost wholly in English air, might have appeared much more to betray a foreign influence" (*TP*, 133). The English foreigner and the foreign Englishwoman—distinctions thus mirrored fail finally to distinguish. The critic can hardly be blamed for the natural inclination to view the Misses Frush as essentially the same.

But moreover, and unfortunately, there is also a modicum of evidence to support the view that the Frushes do differ significantly, at least in the field of their rivalry. Their jealous maneuverings over access to the ghost of Cuthbert Frush will be examined shortly; for now it is enough to note that the seed of their rivalry would seem to be planted by Miss Amy, the more conniving, more vindictive of the pair. Concerning a matter of great importance for our two odd numbers, James tells us this of Miss Amy:

> She had an innocent vanity on the subject of her foot, a member which she somehow regarded as a guarantee of her wit, or at least of her good taste. Even had it not been pretty she flattered herself

it would have been shod: she would never—no, never, like Susan—have given it up. Her bright brown eye was comparatively bold, and she had accepted Susan once for all as a frump. She even thought her, and silently deplored her as, a goose. (*TP,* 134)

Miss Susan, on the contrary, thinks highly of her companion's fashionable air:

They went inveterately to evening church, to the close of which supper was postponed; and Miss Susan, on this occasion, ready the first, patiently awaited her mate at the foot of the stairs. Miss Amy at last came down, buttoning a glove, rustling the tail of a frock and looking, as her kinswoman always thought, conspicuously young and smart. There was no one at Marr, she held, who dressed like her. (*TP,* 146)

But even this distinction is withdrawn almost immediately, folded back upon itself. The passage continues directly: "There was no one at Marr, she held, who dressed like her; and Miss Amy, it must be owned, had also settled to this view of Miss Susan, though taking it in a different spirit" (*TP,* 146). If one attempts to show that Miss Amy is distinguished by her spitefulness, then it must, according to the letter of the text, be demonstrated only in comparison with an equal measure of Miss Susan's ingenuousness.

The result of all this is to land the critic in an uncomfortable and unproductive position. Three possibilities are open to him: viewing the Misses Frush as identical; viewing them as congruent mirror reversals; or viewing one as in some way ascending over the other. Yet the privileging of one of these views over the other two, if only momentarily, for the purpose of constructing a consistent reading of this story, must necessarily remain an arbitrary choice which in turn neglects the efficacy if not the existence of the other competing versions. In such a comparatively simple matter as the describing of characters, the critic approaching "The Third Person" is turned away—penetration coming only at the cost of consistency and linearity—perhaps into biography, or literary history.

II

But with Emerson's dictum on consistency in mind, let us turn back into "The Third Person," to isolate and underline a significant characteristic of and distinction between the two Misses Frush. These esteemed ladies, though living a quiet life, are by no means idlers—each pursues a noble and enriching occupation, even before the advent of their ghost. James's description of these occupations must be quoted at some length:

They had a theory that their lives had been immensely different, and each appeared now to the other to have conducted her career so perversely only that she should have an unfamiliar range of anecdote for her companion's ear. . . . Miss Amy, after all less conventional, at the end of long years of London, abounded in reminiscences of literary, artistic and even—Miss Susan heard it with bated breath—theatrical society, under the influence of which she had written—there, it came out!—a novel that had been anonymously published and a play that had been strikingly type-copied. Not the least charm, clearly, of this picturesque outlook at Marr would be the support that might be drawn from it for getting back, as she hinted, with "general society" bravely sacrificed, to "real work." She had in her head hundreds of plots—with which the future, accordingly, seemed to bristle for Miss Susan. The latter, on her side, was only waiting for the wind to go down to take up again her sketching. . . . Miss Susan came back to English scenery with a small sigh of fondness to which the consciousness of Alps and Apennines only gave more of a quaver; she had picked out her subjects and, with her head on one side and a sense that they were easier abroad, sat sucking her water-colour brush and nervously—perhaps even a little inconsistently—waiting and hesitating. What had happened was that they had, each for herself, re-discovered the country; only Miss Amy, emergent from Bloomsbury lodgings, spoke of it as primroses and sunsets, and Miss Susan, rebounding from the Arno and the Reuss, called it, with a shy, synthetic pride, simply England. (*TP*, 136–37)

However, as this passage clearly shows, the ambitions of the Misses Frush far exceed their abilities. There are simply too many quaverings, too many small fond sighs, on both their parts, to allow us to presume that their productions can in any way match their exalted sensibilities. James's portrayal is persistently and wholly ironic—a gentle poking of fun at the wistful *artiste*.

Neither Miss Amy nor Miss Susan manages to get back to "real work" per se; their attention and their pursuits are deflected into another, albeit related, endeavor. You'll recall that what had happened was that they had rediscovered the "country"—a metaphor that James will employ to achieve a remarkable narrative elision. The passage quoted above continues as follows:

The country was at any rate in the house with them as well as in the little green girdle and in the big blue belt. It was in the objects and relics that they handled together and wondered over, finding in them a ground for much inferred importance and invoked romance, stuffing large stories into very small openings and pulling every faded bell-rope that might jingle rustily into the past. . . . They threw off theories and small imaginations, and almost conceived themselves engaged in researches; all of which made for pomp and circumstance. Their desire was to discover something, and, emboldened by the broader sweep of wing of her companion, Miss Susan herself was not afraid of discovering something bad. (*TP*, 137–38)

What has happened here is that the focus of our couple's occupation has shifted slightly, and in a way that requires some specification. Instead of regarding the elusive "country" as an inspiration for their own creations, the Misses Frush turn to regard this country—now imported *into* their shared house—as an object of "research": they engage in "theories" and "inferences" in the desire to "discover something." The image thus evoked is no longer one of the writer, or of the painter—it is instead a picture of a *reader*. And not a passive and accepting reader, but one who would probe and question, seeking significances; one who could be accused of "stuffing large stories into very small openings." Small wonder then that critics are thrust away from "The Third Person," if they are made to face an almost cruelly parodic image of their *own* enterprise reflected in the mirror of this text.

Still, the country is a large field to cover, and so the ladies narrow their view to a more restricted "text": the ghost of their smuggling ancestor Cuthbert Frush. Naturally, this ghost is a "real" ghost: Miss Susan notes the detail of his twisted neck; only later is it discovered that he had died by hanging; hanged men have twisted necks, etc., etc., Q.E.D. And yet it is interesting to note the peculiar but appropriate difference between the expositions of that ghost's first appearance before each of his respective viewers. Miss Susan receives the first visit:

> "There's some one in my room!"
> They held each other. "But who?"
> "A man."
> "Under the bed?"
> "No—just standing there."
> They continued to hold each other, but they rocked. "Standing? Where? How?"
> "Why, right in the middle—before my dressing-glass."
> Amy's blanched face by this time matched her mate's, but its terror was enhanced by speculation. "To look at himself?"
> "No—with his back to it. To look at *me*," poor Susan just audibly breathed. "To keep me off," she quavered. "In strange clothes—of another age; with his head on one side."
> Amy wondered. "On one side?"
> "Awfully!" the refugee declared while, clinging together, they sounded each other. (*TP*, 141)

Besides the quiet intimation that what Miss Susan has seen is her *own* reflection (since she too is described as, with brush in mouth, having her head "on one side"), it is significant that the reported position of the ghost, in the "middle" of the glass, suggests more than anything else a portrait in a frame. Miss Susan, the hopeful sketcher, offers her testimony in the form of a visually oriented critique. Now, by itself this would seem a tenuous extrapolation upon a tiny detail, until the inevitable comparison with the first visitation suffered by Miss Amy. In search of her prayer book, she ventures into the drawing room; her return, with "something in her movement that spoke," confirms her confrontation by the ghost, reported again in a dialogue of which I quote only the relevant portions:

> "He's there?"
> "Before the fire—with his back to it."
> "Well, now you see!" Miss Susan exclaimed with elation and as if her friend had hitherto doubted her.
> "Yes, I see—and what you mean." Miss Amy was deeply thoughtful.
> "About his head?"
> "It *is* on one side," Miss Amy went on. "It makes him——" she considered. But she faltered as if still in his presence.
> "It makes him awful!" Miss Susan murmured. "The way," she softly moaned, "he looks at you!"

Miss Amy, with a glance, met this recognition. "Yes—doesn't he?" Then her eyes attached themselves to the red windows of the church. "But it means something."

"The Lord knows what it means!" her associate gloomily sighed. . . .

"He's handsome!" Miss Amy brought out after a moment. And she showed herself even prepared to continue: "Splendidly."

"'Splendidly'!—with his neck broken and with that terrible look?"

"It's just the look that makes him so. It's the wonderful eyes. They mean something," Amy Frush brooded. (*TP*, 146–47)

Miss Amy, in turn, and ever the aspiring writer, punctuates her description of her recent encounter with the repeated quest for "meaning" characteristic of the literary critic. Both our ladies, then, and despite any question of the ghost's reality, pursue their relation to him in terms of their own respective methods of critical inquiry.

But might it not be objected that, if the Misses Frush are such assiduous "readers," shouldn't they devote their attention to the deciphering of the ghost's unread letters, rather than to the ghost himself? It is a point well taken. Like so many of James's works—*The Ivory Tower, The Wings of the Dove,* especially "The Turn of the Screw"—"The Third Person" contains "unread" letters. But, while the Misses Frush are unable to penetrate the "Gothic character" they find there, these letters do not remain unread for long: the revelation of their contents is brought by the extraordinary Mr. Patten.

III

The Reverend Mr. Patten is perhaps the most remarkable *ficelle* to be found in all of James's fiction, and the fineness of his rendering is alone enough to recover "The Third Person" from obscurity. The problem of the untrustworthy *ficelle* has been examined at length previously in this study, in my discussion of Mrs. Meldrum in "Glasses," but Mr. Patten presents a much more complex figure. He is not only untrustworthy, but the possibility that he lacks veracity is purposely expounded, in fact paraded, as the pivotal feature of his relation to the two ladies. Mr. Patten, clothed in the respectability naturally accorded a vicar, a respectability only heightened by his position as the town's amateur archivist, is at the same time "a gentleman with a humour of his own": when presented with the baffling letters, he, "at the sight of the papers, exclaimed, perhaps a trifle ambiguously, and by no means clerically, 'My eye, what a lark!' " (*TP*, 140). It is Mr. Patten's "love of a joke" that distinguishes him from Miss Amy, for example, as he reports his findings:

"Mr Cuthbert Frush, it would seem, by name—was hanged."

They never knew afterwards which of the two had first found composure—found even dignity—to respond. "And pray, Mr Patten, for what?"

"Ah, that's just what I don't yet get hold of. But if you don't mind my digging away"—and the vicar's bushy, jolly brows turned from one of the ladies to the other—"I think I can run it to earth.

They hanged, in those days, you know," he added as if he had seen something in their faces, "for almost any trifle!"

"Oh, I hope it wasn't for a trifle!" Miss Susan strangely tittered.

"Yes, of course one would like that, while he was about it—well, it had been, as they say," Mr Patten laughed, "rather for a sheep than for a lamb!"

"Did they hang at that time for a sheep?" Miss Amy wonderingly asked.

It made their friend laugh again. "The question's whether *he* did! But we'll find out." (*TP*, 144)

In the Jamesian world, the failure to understand a joke is an indication of limited sensibility superseded only by the unintentional or unconscious *making* of one. Miss Amy's failure to understand the metaphoric play involved in the old saw of sheep and lambs, her lapse into literality, reveals her as a reader insufficiently able to comprehend the nuances of the text she intends to assault. Both she and Miss Susan are relegated to the roles of grasping, tendentious critics.

And yet, paradoxically, it is Mr. Patten who "authorizes" their critical enterprise, and not merely in his provision of "factual" detail. For the operating "critic" must seek out his "writer," and this is the role prescribed for Mr. Patten. He is admittedly a lover of fictions, as his judgment upon smugglers shows:

"There's nothing at all to be said against them? I quite agree with you," the vicar laughed, "for all my cloth; and I even go so far as to say, shocking as you may think me, that we owe them, in our shabby little shrunken present, the sense of a bustling background, a sort of undertone of romance. They give us"—he humourously kept it up, verging perilously near, for his cloth, upon positive paradox—"our little handful of legend and our small possibility of ghosts." (*TP*, 148–49)

But his role is not confined to one of a mere aficionado of fictional forms: he is a dabbler, of sorts, in their production. Upon hearing Miss Amy's expression of agreement, and her avowal that she too would defraud the revenue, he shares with her the following extraordinary dialogue:

Their visitor, at this, amused and amusing, eagerly seized her arm. "Then may I count on you on the stroke of midnight to help me——?"

"To help you——?"

"To land the last new Tauchnitz."

She met the proposal as one whose fancy had kindled, while her cousin watched them as if they had suddenly improvised a drawing-room charade. "A service of danger?"

"Under the cliff—when you see the lugger stand in!"

"Armed to the teeth?"

"Yes—but invisibly. Your old waterproof——!"

"Mine is new. I'll take Susan's!"

This good lady, however, had her reserves. "Mayn't one of them, all the same—here and there—have been sorry?"

Mr Patten wondered, "For the jobs he muffed?" (*TP*, 149–50)

What is taking place in this conversation is a tiny attempt at the construction of a *plot,* a scenario. At Patten's instigation, Miss Amy responds in the joint rehearsal of the familiar form of the romance, and it is a diversion absorbing enough to cause Patten to deliver not the vicar's condemnation of a crime, but the humorist's condemnation of a deficiency in its commission.

If Mr. Patten makes the contents of the letters patently clear, then it might also be said that, as he returns their bundle, he issues them with a set of letters patent, an authorization to proceed on their chosen enterprise. And yet it is an authorization suffused in irony, and undermined by humor. Their master storyteller is a joker, a teller of tall tales; they are his unworthy dupes. The essence of their relation is revealed to us by James in the following droll passage:

> "Ah, but we want the truth!" they cried with high emphasis as he quitted them. They were much excited now.
>
> He answered by pulling up and turning round as short as if his professional character had been challenged. "Isn't it just in the truth—and the truth only—that I deal?"
>
> This they recognized as much as his love of a joke, and so they were left there together in the pleasant, if slightly overdone, void of the square. (*TP,* 145)

It is not the determination of "truth" that is in question here; rather, it is the figure of an author presumably in control of a truth knowingly and openly standing that truth on its head, making it into a joke. The result is that both the pursuer of that truth and the pursuit itself, critic and criticism alike, are thwarted.

The gaily delivered admonitions of Mr. Patten go unheeded, however, and the Misses Frush blithely continue to heap their constructions upon the "third person in their association" (*TP,* 142). These constructions, their readings of the "hovering presence," are soon seen to follow one particular and precise line of inquiry. Receiving the letters back from Mr. Patten, Miss Amy takes charge of the treasure: "She placed the tattered papers piously together, wrapping them tenderly in a piece of old figured silken stuff; then, as solemnly as if they had been archives or statutes or title-deeds, laid them away in one of the several small cupboards lodged in the thickness of the wainscoted walls" (*TP,* 152). And it is significant to note that, following directly upon this act of enshrinement, the narration shifts focus to the prospect of their importance:

> What really most sustained our friends in all ways was their consciousness of having, after all—and so contrariwise to what appeared—a man in the house. It removed them from that category of the manless into which no lady really lapses till every issue is closed. Their visitor was an issue—at least to the imagination, and they arrived finally, under provocation, at intensities of flutter in which they felt themselves so compromised by his hoverings that they could only consider with relief the fact of nobody's knowing. (*TP,* 152)

Thus we find that the ghost will serve our two ladies as the recipient of their projected and mutual sexual fantasies—those "intensities of flutter" will only increase in duration and frequency. The approach of such a delicate subject is of course tentative, as befits a pair who would rank as worse than murder the possibility of "gay deception" (*TP,* 138). But the tension does mount, and candor increase, from Miss Amy's appreciation of the ghost's handsomeness, through Miss Susan's nocturnal interview while clad only in her wrapper (!), to their joint recognition of mutual jealousy. The twisted course of their competition and rivalry is too evident to the reader of this tale, and forms too large a portion of it, to warrant repetition here. What is important to recognize, however, is that their rivalry is such that each repeatedly and successively seeks to take precedence over the other vis-à-vis the ghost: who gets more visits, longer visits, "deeper" visits—these are the crucial points of contention. What the reader witnesses finally is that each woman attempts to define her relationship to the ghost according to her own primacy—the ghost himself becomes only a plastic presence, molded to fit the contours of her desires. Or to hop from one metaphor to another, our two fledgling critics, in their attack on the as yet unread text before them, hasten to establish a critical claim there that would finally disallow any competing, differing readings. The remarks of Shoshana Felman, made while enmeshed in the intricacies of "The Turn of the Screw," are not inapposite here:

> The comprehension ("grasp," "reach his mind") of the meaning the Other is presumed to know, which constitutes the ultimate aim of any act of reading, is thus conceived as a violent gesture of appropriation, a gesture of domination of the Other. Reading, in other words, establishes itself as a relation not only to *knowledge* but equally to *power*; it consists not only of a search for meaning but also of a struggle to control it.[5]

Both Miss Amy and Miss Susan, each lost in the bizarre enactment of her own desire, fight to appropriate the text they read in order to construct, in short, their own personal "romance." The power they pursue is thus not merely the power to achieve their desires, but the power to define and control the bounds of the narrative that encloses that desire—even if it happens to belong to Henry James. But, as we come to see, this is a power that James expressly refuses to grant.

IV

Much has been made of the painstakingly constructed narrative "frame" to be found in the prologue to "The Turn of the Screw." Indeed, many critics have employed this frame, and its concomitant implications regarding the deferral and distancing of authority, as a launching point for their own critical sallies.

It should be noted if only in passing that such a reading of the prologue depends for the most part on a bit of critical fictionalizing. Since the employment of such disclaimers of authorship is a familiar fictive device (to the point of suffering parodic treatment at the hands of, for example, John Barth or Umberto

Eco), one must assume an unfamiliarity with the conventions of fiction almost to the point of precluding critical response in order *not* to perceive that such a framing does not distance authority, but instead emphasizes it, in the form of the comparative beauty of its execution. But whether one accepts the frame through naivete or through the suspension of disbelief, the effect is much the same—the frame displaces the author at least to the extent that it makes room for a reader.

I raise this point regarding "The Turn of the Screw" in order to point out that "The Third Person" has no such prologue, and no such frame. And more than this, this absence is not a mere omission, but the indication of a conscious withdrawal of the room for "reading" granted by the frame. The title of "The Third Person" refers of course to the ghost of Cuthbert Frush:

> There had been something hitherto wanting, they felt, to their small state and importance; it was present now, and they were as handsomely conscious of it as if they had previously missed it. The element in question, then, was a third person in their association, a hovering presence for the dark hours, a figure that with its head very much —too much—on one side, could be trusted to look at them out of unnatural places; yet only, it doubtless might be assumed, to look at them. (*TP*, 142)

But "the third person" refers as well to a particular mode of narration, a fictional form implying exteriority, omniscience, and the fullest measure of authorial control. Unlike "The Turn of the Screw," "The Third Person" is written in "the third person," and we do not encounter a reasonably detached and impartial narrator here, but one who indulges himself in repeated and ironic commentary on the foibles of his creations. The instances of authorial intrusion into the flow of this narrative are too numerous to bear citation; indeed, they account for much of the abundant humor to be found in this story. Perhaps my reader would do well to review some of the passages quoted above, with the assurance that the authorial commentary readily discerned there is not atypical of the text in its entirety. Then again, one further example may be useful. Early in the story, James reports the judgment of Miss Amy upon Miss Susan: "She had accepted Susan once for all as a frump. She even thought her, and silently deplored her as, a goose" (*TP*, 134). It is a judgment immediately judged, as James concludes the paragraph with the following: "But she was none the less herself a lamb" (*TP*, 134). In this small yet striking metaphoric play, we cannot fail to be aware that, if either of the ladies would pride herself on her theories, or seek to gain the upper hand on her counterpart, her maneuvers are always already circumscribed by the superior hand of the third person narrator. Her attempts at critical reading are anticipated, weighed, and duly dismissed; her desires for power are not permitted to impinge upon the designs of the Master.

Precious little room is left for the reader of the third person, or of "The Third Person," precluded by a text that would incorporate and simultaneously nullify its own criticism. But such a harsh treatment of the hopeful critic is not without its echoes elsewhere in James. In the portion of the Prefaces dealing with "The Turn of the Screw," as we have already noted, James specifically refers to that text as having a perfect and independent resistance to "sharp" questions, with its "conscious provision of prompt retort" to them (*AN,* 169). What is most interesting here is that, despite his earnest avowal on this point, James expends much of the remainder of his discussion in a defense of "The Turn of the Screw" against sharp critical questions: namely, the accusation of an excess of "evil" in the story, and the charge that the governess is insufficiently "characterized." The substance of James's retort to these criticisms is unimportant here; instead, it is his tone that we must consider. The latter of these comments is made, we are told, "by a reader capable evidently, for the time, of some attention, but not quite capable of enough . . . " (*AN,* 173). One need hardly emphasize that, for James, an inattentive reader is an unworthy critic, and his judgments are not to be countenanced. Thus the air of high mock seriousness pervading James's reply to this criticism, "under which one's artistic, one's ironic heart shook for the instant almost to breaking" (*AN,* 173), in a lengthy disquisition that concludes with this rough dismissal of such a view of the governess:

> We have surely as much of her own nature as we can swallow in watching it reflect her anxieties and inductions. It constitutes no little of a character indeed, in such conditions, for a young person, as she says, "privately bred," that she is able to make her particular credible statement of such strange matters. She has "authority," which is a good deal to have given her, and I couldn't have arrived at so much had I clumsily tried for more. (*AN,* 174)

Of course, the concluding reference to the "authority" granted the governess can only reflect back upon the one who has that authority to give; with it James fires his departing volley at the carping critic. And if the transference of that narrative authority results merely in the nagging queries of a foolish reader, how surprising is it that in "The Third Person," a story expressly addressed to such readers, authority is neither forthcoming, nor "given" to anyone, but is instead retained and exercised?

It is the final exercise of that authority that returns us again to the Misses Frush. These besieged critics have by now reached a point where their attempts to wrest control from each other, and from James, have turned naturally to the question of how to *end* their curious romance. As James informs us: "What was definite was that they had lived into their queer story, passed through it as through an observed, a studied, eclipse of the usual, a period of reclusion, a financial, social or moral crisis, and only desired now to live out of it again" (*TP,* 163). But their dependence on the methods of reading again betrays their failure as writers: "The great questions remained. What then did he mean? what then did he want? Absolution, peace, rest, his final reprieve—merely to say *that* saw them no further on the way than they had already come. What were they at last to do for him? What could they give him that he would take?" (*TP*, 163). Armed only with a series of questions—the critic's stock in trade—the Misses Frush are unable to finally obtain the control of the narrative necessary to exorcise their personal ghost. This explains why, when resolving their mutual jealousy, the determination not to argue over a man until there actually *is* a man is alone insufficient to achieve their aim: the shift in the ghost's "ontological" status indicates merely a shift in interpretative focus, without discarding the fundamental basis of their enterprise—the method of reading that produces the romance they now wish to end. Nor can Miss Susan's attempt to atone for their ancestor's sins through the offering of "conscience-money" to the Exchequer banish their visitor, as its conception depends as well on the necessary assumptions underlying their fiction. Only an excursion "outside" the bounds of their text will bring success; and it is here that the daring adventure of Miss Amy must be recounted, albeit at some length:

"He's gone. And how," she insisted, "*did* you do it?"

"Why, you dear goose"—Miss Amy spoke a little strangely—"I went to Paris."

"To Paris?"

"To see what I could bring back—that I mightn't, that I shouldn't. To do a stroke with!" Miss Amy brought out.

But it left her friend still vague. "A stroke——?"

"To get through the Customs—under their nose."

It was only with this that, for Miss Susan, a pale light dawned. "You wanted to smuggle? *That* was your idea?"

"It was *his*," said Miss Amy. "He wanted no 'conscience money' spent for him," she now more bravely laughed: "it was quite the other way about—he wanted some bold deed done, of the old wild kind; he wanted some big risk taken. And I took it." She sprang up, rebounding, in her triumph.

Her companion, gasping, gazed at her. "Might they have hanged you too?"

Miss Amy looked up at the dim stars. "If I had defended myself. But luckily it didn't come to that. What I brought in I brought"—she rang out, more and more lucid, now, as she talked—"triumphantly. To appease him—I braved them. I chanced it, at Dover, and they never knew."

"Then you hid it——?"

"About my person."

With the shiver of this Miss Susan got up, and they stood there duskily together. "It was so small?" the elder lady wonderingly murmured.

"It was big enough to have satisfied him," her mate replied with just a shade of sharpness. "I chose it, with much thought, from the forbidden list."

The forbidden list hung a moment in Miss Susan's eyes, suggesting to her, however, but a pale conjecture. "A Tauchnitz?"

Miss Amy communed again with the August stars. "It was the *spirit* of the deed that told."

"A Tauchnitz?" her friend insisted.

Then at last her eyes again dropped, and the Misses Frush moved together to the house. "Well, he's satisfied."

"Yes, and"—Miss Susan mused a little ruefully as they went—"you got at last your week in Paris!" (*TP*, 168–69)

Miss Amy's exorcism is in fact successful—the ghost has fled—though the precise method by which she achieved it remains somewhat ambiguous. Was the forbidden object in fact a Tauchnitz? The answer to this question is withheld, and the contraband not specified (and here it might be wondered whether the withholding of crucial information is for Miss Amy a sign of achieved authority or merely one more instance of protecting a private horde), but the suggestion of the Tauchnitz cannot fail to be significant, inasmuch as this is precisely the forbidden object chosen for the center of Mr. Patten's romantic tale.

The passage above is rich in humor, as numerous strands of this story reemerge. The reference to the "goose," the intimation of sweetly forbidden carnality implied in hiding an object about one's "person," the echoes of the "forbidden list," the recaptured shudders and thrills of two spinsters relating a tale under the August stars—all these contribute to an air of ironic distance that allows for James's capping joke regarding the Tauchnitz. This "bold deed" of the "old wild kind"—the smuggling through Customs of a Continental edition of an English author, without paying the duty that would compensate that author—is no doubt to the readers of "The Third Person" a comparatively paltry affair. Its commission, and the way in which the pair rhapsodizes over Miss Amy's tiny crime, reveals more than anything else their restricted range of experience, their essential and unassailable naivete. Charming though they may be, the Misses Frush are to the last, as James firmly reminds us, a goose and a lamb.

But the joke regarding the Tauchnitz extends one crucial step further, and with that step moves from the amusing to the outlandish. It is, quite simply, this: James himself was published in Tauchnitz editions. In point of fact, considering only the period up to 1900, some *thirty* of James's novels, collections of tales and travel books were issued by the Leipzig house of Bernhard Tauchnitz. The reader of "The Third Person," then, must exit this short story with the extraordinary intuition that a character in a Henry James story ends that story with the importation of yet *another* Henry James story.[6]

The implications of this are manifold. If we recall that the control of authorship is essentially a power play, that the critical reader seeks to control the fiction through a process of reading that explains and renders consistent that fiction, some sort of fictive deferral of that authority is necessary for entry to be possible. In "The Third Person," however, such authority is *not* deferred, but is purposefully and aggressively reasserted: the final reference to the Tauchnitz James signals that, for Miss Amy and for us, attempts to control exist only to the extent that they are allowed—wresting away authority is by definition an impossibility. The smuggling of the Tauchnitz is an evasion of one authority—the customs, the duty collector —but what that evasion covers, and disguises, is the persistence of authority in the figure of Henry James the Master, himself in the disguise of a Tauchnitz. The best Miss Amy can do is to buy the book—James himself will write it, and "The Third Person" as well.

Thus we can see the need not to name James here, as the author of the Tauchnitz. What this provides for is the possibility of Miss Amy's fondly desired "week in Paris," the Jamesian capital of passionate intrigue, seemingly outside the borders of ordinary control. Still, it is a visit with a predetermined purpose, not a Pattenesque "lark," and is limited to a week—a mere vacation from the prescribed norms of behavior. Even here, alas, there is no escape.

Much, much more than "The Turn of the Screw," "The Third Person" is, in James's words, "a piece of ingenuity pure and simple, of cold artistic calculation, an *amusette* to catch those not easily caught" (*AN*, 172).

V

If my reading of "The Third Person" seems contrived, overly optimistic, or otherwise unsatisfactory, I plead no contest. What could one expect from a text that will not be "read"? It embodies its own critics, its own criticism, and its own "criticism" of its criticism, and delivers them all back in the sardonic voice of the meta-fictionist. It has resisted my approaches, denied my rights as reader, laughed at me. I am content to let my critical text die here, stillborn, and seek with my colleagues the comparative safety of the historian.

As noted at the outset of this chapter, "The Third Person" appears to receive no mention in Henry James's Notebooks—at least none that his critics have been able to locate. I quite agree that no specific reference to a story with that title appears there; nor is there reference to a "ghost story" which might fit the general contours of this one. And yet, there is in the Notebooks a most curious series of references comprising the vague outlines of a story never written—perhaps.

What came to be tentatively titled "The Publisher's Story" makes its first appearance in the Notebooks on November 18, 1894:

> Isn't there perhaps the subject of a little—a very little—tale (*de moeurs littéraires*) in the idea of a man of letters, a poet, a novelist, finding out, after years, or a considerable period, of very happy, unsuspecting, and more or less affectionate, intercourse with a 'lady-writer,' a newspaper woman, as it were, that he has been systematically *débiné*, 'slated' by her in certain critical journals to which she contributes? He has known her long and liked her, known of her hack-work, etc., and liked it less; and has also known that the *éreintements* in question have periodically appeared—but he has never connected them with her or her with them, and when he makes the discovery it is an agitating, a very painful, revelation to him. Or the reviewer may be a man and the author anonymously and viciously—or, at least, abusively—reviewed may be a woman. The point of the thing is whether there be not a little supposable theme or drama in the relation, the situation of the two people after the thing comes to light—the pretension on the part of the reviewer of having one attitude to the writer *as* a writer, and a totally distinct one as a member of society, a friend, a human being. They *may* be—the reviewer may be—unconsciously, disappointedly, *rég[u]lièrement*, in love with the victim. It is only a little situation; but perhaps there is something in it. (*NB*, 107–8)

Without question, there are numerous elements in this outline that will not mesh with "The Third Person" as ultimately constituted, but I am intrigued by those traces that do. Note especially the fundamental distinction here between the superiority of the "man of letters" and the mere "hack-work" of the "lady-writer," and the underlying conflict constructed on the basis of unfair criticisms, or "slatings." The zealous endeavors of the Misses Frush slowly begin to take shape.

James returns to his consideration of "The Publisher's Story" on December 21, 1895:

> The reviewing woman who *éreinters* her friend—the man of letters who comes to see her—in the paper for which she does novels, *because she is RAGEUSEMENT* in love with him. The publisher finds it out—it might be called *The Publisher's Story*. There must be, of course, some climax: the idea must be: '*What is the way to make her stop?*' 'Try a sweet review of her, and let her know it's yours.' 'But I hate her work.' 'Well, nevertheless, pump out something.' The novelist tries this—it has no effect.—I check myself: there may be something in the *concetto* (a very small something indeed—even for 5000 words), but it doesn't lie in that direction. *Laissons cela* till something more seems to come out of it. (*NB,* 147)

Here, the relative inferiority of the woman's work is further emphasized, as is her condition as a failed fictionist as well as a hack critic. As well, the notion of putting an end to this irritation emerges as the focal point: "*What is the way to make her stop?*" The importation of the publisher suggests the intermediary agency of the Tauchnitz, another publisher.

Once more, this time on May 7, 1898:

> 'The Publisher's Story.' Mrs. X.—a literary woman—EREINTERS *pendant de longues années* a writer—preferably novelist or poet. I (the Publisher) ask: 'Why can't you let him alone? You *know* him—like him.' 'Yes, but I don't like his work.' Then—about his never seeing what she says: *elle est rageuse*. I put my finger on the place: 'You love him.' She has to admit it. 'Well, try another tack.' She writes a eulogy, which he *sees*; and learns the authorship of, and in consequence of which he does notice her work. X X X X X I see the *other* woman or girl, who, then, on the accident of his seeing at last the back numbers and learning who *has* slated him (it needn't have been for so long; a year or two) says '*I* wrote them'; to save her friend. But *my* thought, on this, of how *she,* the 2d girl, must love. (*NB,* 169–70)

Further traces emerge. Note first the shift in emphasis from the Author to the Publisher, and the explicit application of the "I" there—as well as the plaintive inquiry of "Why can't you let him alone?" Here the notion of a higher and more exalted authority begins to solidify, as well as that authority's confrontation with and rejection of the offending critic. Note as well the heretofore unmentioned second woman, and her role as a pretender to the authorship of the first.

"The Publisher's Story" seems to have haunted James more diligently than Cuthbert Frush haunted his descendants. For some five years he retained the basic thread of the story, returning to it for the fourth and final time on February 14,

1899: "And for the Publisher's story, revert to what I seem to have (in this vol.) got hold of the tail of—the idea of the 2d woman (girl), who falsely takes upon *herself* the authorship of the 'slatings' and who is *the* one that the narrator attributes the secret passion to" (*NB*, 176). Admittedly, an assertion that "The Publisher's Story" ultimately metamorphosed into "The Third Person" must stand largely without support, especially if my reading of the latter is not accepted. Still, the possibility is intriguing, especially in light of another brief and apparently unrelated entry in the Notebooks, dated at about the time "The Third Person" would have been written: " 'The Sketcher'—some little drama, situation, complication, fantasy, to be worked into small Rye-figure of woman working away (on my doorstep and elsewhere)" (*NB*, 184). I must leave it to my reader to decide whether the "little drama" needed here will turn out to be "The Publisher's Story," and whether it will further evolve into "The Third Person." This much, however, seems clear: this small Rye-figure of a woman, whether Susan or Amy Frush, or neither, is welcome on the doorstep of Lamb House only on the express invitation of the Master.

6

Yet Another Artful Dodger: "Collaboration"

As my reader will perhaps have noted, each of the short stories previously addressed here shares the common property of centering upon the adventures of a sort of *sotto voce* writer. Though cloaked in more conventional fictive pursuits—the international theme, tales of lost love and revenge, the ghost story—each reveals itself to be concerned in large part with the mechanisms of authority that ultimately license authorship, or "art." It is as though we have been sketching the outlines of a competing collection, an "unauthorized" edition, if you will, of Henry James's stories of writers and artists. But if the questions of authorship and creation are tacit in these fictions, it remains for us to turn to a story in which they become undeniably manifest.

I

"Collaboration," written in 1892, had received next to no critical attention until Adeline Tintner's brief analytic essay in 1983.[1] Leon Edel terms it "one of Henry's trifling and artful anecdotes," and provides if unwittingly what may be an explanation for its canonical exclusion.[2] Employing "Collaboration" as a reflection of James's entanglement with Constance Fenimore Woolson, particularly in regard to Fenimore's suggestion that they collaborate in the writing of a play, Edel explains James's apparent refusal to do so by an analysis of the author's most deeply held beliefs on the nature of artistic creation: "He was, in all of his writing years, an arch-solitary of literature. He took no guidance; he consulted no one—although he talked freely enough about the problems of the marketplace. He would have regarded collaboration as an abandoning of sovereign ground, the most sacred ground of his life."[3] The "sovereign" and the "sacred": once more the inviolate integrity of the Master asserts itself. Set apart from the crowd by an act of self-will, immune to outside influence (especially the influence of lesser lights), the Master constitutes himself in singleness, on the basis of an inviolable and carefully circumscribed unity of authorship. Collaboration, then, is anathema, for it involves a dissemination of authorship, a blurring of origins in which responsibility can no longer be reliably traced. The Master may have disciples in legion, but no partners: corporate authorship is inimical to authority.

Might it not therefore be the case that "Collaboration" stands outside the Jamesian canon simply because it takes collaboration as its subject, and takes it seriously as such? In other words, this fiction focuses on an instance of creative collaboration, indeed exalting it above mere political or social concerns, but since collaboration is inconsonant with the portrayal of James the Master, "Collaboration" must be rejected. The argument, though neat, is finally unpersuasive. For example, in one of James's most celebrated tales, "The Figure in the Carpet," the relation between George Corvick and Gwendolen Erme is essentially collaborative. In fact, as I argued earlier, their quest for the secret of Hugh Vereker's work is largely unsuccessful until they engage in this collaboration, which in turn becomes sanctified through their marriage and sustained by Erme's fidelity even after her husband's death. Of course, it could be objected that it is Vereker's status as the prototypical fictive "Master" that counterweighs their corporate venture, but it must be remembered that both mastery and collaboration are circumscribed there by "The Figure in the Carpet"'s unnamed narrator, damned as he is to that specifically Jamesian hell reserved for the clever and the egotistical. Mastery in that tale is routed back to Henry James, in his manipulation of the disparate strands of the narrative, one of which is undeniably the presentation of a collaborative venture. Thus, the expulsion of "Collaboration" from the Jamesian canon cannot be due solely to its subject matter, since elsewhere "collaboration" has been treated without objection or even remark. The reasons for this tale's exclusion lie elsewhere, within the fabric of the text itself.

Taken as a "story," "Collaboration" is admittedly slight. Félix Vendemer, a young French poet, meets Herman Heidenmauer, a young German composer. Thoroughly taken with each other's artistry, they agree to collaborate on an opera. Their decision is not without dramatic effects, however, since, coming on the heels of the Franco-Prussian war, it carries political implications beyond the bounds of joint creative endeavor. Vendemer's fiancée Paule de Brindes repudiates their engagement, Heidenmauer's funds are cut off by his brother, the whole of Paris society apparently unites in rejection and disgust, and we leave the pair in retreat in Italy, penniless and feverishly engaged in their "monstrous" collaboration. Even this small measure of "action" is muted, however, by the narrative's reliance on implication and prediction rather than exposition. We are left instead with a series of pronouncements on the ascendancy of "Art" over politics, pronouncements which become increasingly preachy in tone.

It is appropriate that the topic of these sermons should be the nature and function of Art, since without exception each and every character in

"Collaboration" is in some way or another an artist. Vendemer is a poet, Heidenmauer a musician, Paule de Brindes "has a happy turn for keeping a water-colour liquid," while her mother Madame de Brindes, employed largely in the story as the exemplar of French chauvinism, "plies an ingenious, pathetic pen" as the authoress of "touching tales" appearing between "pretty lemon-coloured covers."[4] Even such a minor character as the American Alfred Bonus (immediately identifiable as an instance of a familiar Jamesian type—the clever and clutching yet obviously limited hanger-on) enters this circle of artists in the role of the critic-correspondent, "whose occupation was to write letters to the American journals about the way the 'boys' were coming on in Paris" (*CO*, 409). The result of this casting is not only to place the question of collaborative artistry squarely within a community comprised exclusively of artists: as my enumeration indicates, by the assignment of specified artistic pursuits to each of the characters in this tale, James has drawn clearly defined lines between separable and discrete artistic genres. Each of his characters has his or her own artistic bailiwick, each chases his own personal muse to one degree of success or another, each possesses an area of expertise clearly distinguished from every other—each character, that is, save one.

Granville H. Jones's brief synopsis of "Collaboration" is notable in that it mistakenly identifies the narrator of this tale as Alfred Bonus. Such a mistake becomes important in that, instead of being a simple instance of misreading, it brings to the fore the crucial question of "Collaboration"—the question of the narrator's identity and status. "Collaboration" is a first-person narrative and, as is the case as well in "Glasses," full entry into this text comes only with the recognition of the difficulties of its narrative form. Those critics who have addressed this story have for the most part overlooked the narrator, concentrating instead upon the dilemma of Félix Vendemer. Such a strategy of reading does not, however, constitute merely a case of critical omission. On the contrary, it seems that it is a necessary reaction to a mode of narration that is especially opaque, and to a narrator who would remain essentially indeterminate throughout. This narrator, who also remains unnamed throughout, takes great pains to introduce himself to his readers:

> I don't know how much people care for my work, but they like my studio (of which indeed I am exceedingly fond myself), as they show by their inclination to congregate there at dusky hours on winter afternoons, or on long dim evenings when the place looks well with its rich combinations and low-burning lamps and the bad pictures (my own) are not particularly visible. I won't go into the question of how many of these are purchased, but I rejoice in the distinction that my invitations are never declined. (*CO*, 407)

In these first few lines of "Collaboration," we find that the narrator is a painter, and thus shares with his fellows the designation of "artist." But it is a label immediately withdrawn, both by the prompt relegation of his productions to darkness and insignificance, and by the deflection of attention from the works themselves to the place of their production, which in turn becomes not a studio as such, but a kind of salon, a gathering place for other artists. The narrator's description of his studio is lengthy, and his fondness for it borders on the fatuous, but portions of that description are revealing:

> The place is really a chamber of justice, a temple of reconciliation: we understand each other if we only sit up late enough. Art protects her children in the long run—she only asks them to trust her. She is like the Catholic Church—she guarantees paradise to the faithful. Music moreover is a universal solvent; though I've not an infallible ear I've a sufficient sense of the matter for that. Ah, the wounds I've known it to heal—the bridges I've known it to build—the ghosts I've known it to lay! Though I've seen people stalk out I've never observed them not to steal back. My studio in short is the theatre of a cosmopolite drama, a comedy essentially "of character." (*CO*, 408)

Aside from the reporting of social niceties, this passage is noteworthy for the way in which ordinarily distinct artistic genres become mixed, blended: the studio of a painter is converted variously into concert hall and stage, not to mention the references to chamber and church.[5] In contrast to the assignment of discrete artistic realms to each of the other characters, our narrator refuses to allow himself to be captured by any such limited designation. By defining himself exclusively in relation to his studio, and construing that studio as the mixing pot of various artistic forms, the narrator manages to secure for himself a place outside any and all of these forms, artfully sliding back and forth between them and eluding attempts to pin him down. Instead, he acts as a sort of panderer to tastes, making sure that "the piano, the tobacco and the tea are all of the best" (*CO*, 407), and as a kind of neutral site on which the diagnoses of politics and art can be played out.

It would be going too far to ascribe to this narrator the role of mediator, however: though he does function as a sort of intermediary between Madame de Brindes and Vendemer, and between Vendemer and Heidenmauer, his ministrations are for the most part passive and inconsequential—it is enough simply to acquaint the two young men with each other's works, and to provide them with a place to meet. As Vendemer anguishes over the proposal made by Heidenmauer, well aware of its implications and its possible effect on his plans for marriage, the narrator prepares to leave Vendemer for a dinner engagement, offering only this response to his friend's pain:

> I laughed, to Vendemer, partly with a really amused sense of the exaggerated woe that looked out of hispoetic eyes and that seemed an appeal to me not to forsake him, to throw myself into the scale of the associations he would have to stifle, and partly to encourage him, to express my conviction that two such fine minds couldn't in the long run be the worse for coming to an agreement. I might have been a more mocking Mephistopheles handing over his pure spirit to my literally German Faust. (*CO*, 424)

The concluding reference to Faust adds but one more turn of the screw—the importation of the literary arts into the already crowded repertoire of our narrator/dilettante.

II

It is as a writer that we must now consider the narrator, especially in terms of his portrait of Madame de Brindes. The latter, widowed in the Franco-Prussian war and impoverished by the fall of the Empire, stands resolute as the pillar of French nationalism: it is her abhorrence of all things German that underscores the perversity of the subsequent collaboration. But she is also aware of the contingencies of finance—as the narrator informs us, "vulgar is what she tries hard to be, she is so convinced it is the only way to make a living" (*CO*, 412–13). In describing both her and her daughter, the narrator tells us: "There is something exquisite in the way these ladies are earnestly, conscientiously modern. From the moment they accept necessities they accept them all, and poor Madame de Brindes flatters herself that she has made her dowerless daughter one of us others" (*CO*, 412). This cryptic phrase—"one of us others"—resounds throughout this text, utterly immune to definition. Who are "us others"? Can it be those not French? Not "modern"? No clue is forthcoming, though the phrase reappears in the very next paragraph. Félix Vendemer, we are told, "simply fell in love with Mademoiselle de Brindes and behaved, on his side, equally like one of us others" (*CO*, 412). Again a distinction is made that remains curiously indistinct. Vendemer, now too "one of us others," would like to marry Paule de Brindes, but his financial state interferes: "A volume of verse was a scanty provision to marry on, so that, still like a pair of us others, the luckless lovers had to bide their time" (*CO*, 413). This thrice-repeated reference to "one of us others" simply cannot be nailed down. What its appearance does is call attention to the act of categorizing that underlies its employment. Madame de Brindes is thoroughly French, Heidenmauer thoroughly German, Bonus thoroughly American—but the narrator, ever adroit, avoids these conventional separations. Emptied of its content, the designation of nationality is revealed as just one more instance of choosing up sides, of deciding who is "us" and who is "one of the others"—*ces gens-là*. Art, on the other hand, offers the hope of transcending these paltry distinctions—or so we are told.

Unfortunately (at least for the reader who would like to square "Collaboration" with the image of James the Master), the curious phrase "one of us others" echoes forth one further time in this text. Félix Vendemer is the source of most of the high-minded disquisitions on Art to be found in this tale—his most fervent declamation occurs in a conversation with the narrator immediately following the making of his pact with his collaborator:

"It will cost me everything!" said Félix Vendemer in a tone I seem to hear at this hour. "That's just the beauty of it. It's the chance of chances to testify for art—to affirm an indispensible truth."

"An indispensible truth?" I repeated, feeling myself soar too, but into the splendid vague.

"Do you know the greatest crime that can be perpetrated against it?"

"Against it?" I asked, still soaring.

"Against the religion of art—against the love for beauty—against the search for the Holy Grail?" The transfigured look with which he named these things, the way his warm voice filled the rich room, was a revelation of the wonderful talk that had taken place.

"Do you know—for one of *us*—the really damnable, the only unpardonable, sin?"

"Tell me, so that I may keep clear of it!"

"To profane *our* golden air with the hideous invention of patriotism."

"It was a clever invention in its time!" I laughed. (*CO*, 425)

Here, in the midst of an attack upon the unfair restrictions of nationalism, the artist is reduced to employing the same techniques of restriction, the same mechanisms of categorization and exclusion that characterize the patriot. Note well how even the "golden air" is owned, as Vendemer speaks of this unpardonable sin—for "one of *us*."

Félix Vendemer's use of the betraying "one of us" raises a most disturbing question. Can it be possible that the notion of Art transcendent is struck down here by the remorseless irony of the narrator? That is to say, if the crude categorizing of the nationalist is to be eschewed, how then are we to redeem the ameliorative claims made for "art" in this text, when their chief exponent Vendemer engages in his own hasty categorizations? The narrator's laughs ring loudly in our ears. Are we to reread "Collaboration" from the reverse angle, wherein even appeals to the Muse are relentlessly ironic? It is an horrific possibility, involving no less than the overthrow of all that is presumably sacred to Henry James the Master.

Yet face the possibility we must. One final passage of this text needs to emerge: in it, Vendemer, Bonus and the narrator discuss their favorite subject. Vendemer speaks first and loudest:

"I don't know what is meant by French art and English art and American art: those seem to me mere cataloguers' and reviewers' and tradesmen's names, representing preoccupations utterly foreign to the artist. Art is art in every country, and the novel (since Bonus mentions that) is the novel in every tongue, and hard enough work they have to live up to that privilege, without our adding another muddle to the problem. The reader, the consumer may call things as he likes, but we leave him to his little amusements." I suggested that we were all readers and consumers; which only made Vendemer continue: "Yes, and only a small handful of us have the ghost of a palate. But you and I and Bonus are of the handful."

"What do you mean by the handful?" Bonus inquired.

Vendemer hesitated a moment. "I mean the few intelligent people, and even the few people who are not——" He paused again an instant, long enough for me to request him not to say what they were "not," and then went on: "People in a word who have the honour to live in the only country worth living in."

"And pray what country is that?"

"The land of dreams—the country of art."

"Oh, the land of dreams! I live in the land of realities!" Bonus exclaimed. (*CO*, 416–17)

That Vendemer privileges a select few ("a small handful *of us*") is not surprising—it is the composition of that few that alarms. Alfred Bonus exists in "Collaboration" as little more than a provincial idiot—he mistakes Heidenmauer's nationality, engages in argument with him over the relative merit of English writing on the basis of that mistake, fails to discern the quality of the narrator's paintings, and writes for an audience not particularly interested. Vendemer's inclusion of Bonus in his select handful of art's initiates cannot be written off to conversational decorum—it militates far too strongly against the notion that Vendemer's elect are somehow better than their "enemies."

The qualifications for membership in this elite handful are not specified—it is the narrator who sees to that. The narrator of "Collaboration" is of course "unreliable," but he is not just unreliable: his status within this text is, paradoxically enough, defined precisely by his indeterminacy. All the "events" in this fiction swim in his ironic relation—which accounts finally for the sense of uneventfulness that pervades the story. The narrator's stance regarding the collaboration is the pivotal point of this text, not the collaboration itself; and with the indeterminacy of that relation before us, we as readers of "Collaboration" are left without a clear point of entry or exit. Attempts at mastery, even by a reader, are precluded, and an ironic play with the established categories of artistic creation and response is placed in their stead.

One final inference must be traced. The collaboration between Vendemer and Heidenmauer is constituted in large part on the basis of its "criminal" status—only against the resistance of lesser sensibilities can their work emerge as the product of a triumphant sacrifice. But with the ironization of the principles underlying their project, little room seems to be left for creation. Can the artist's only site consist in the precarious balancing of ironies?

It is a question our narrator does not answer. And yet, his final words are not inappropriate here. With the two young artists lodged on the Genoese Riviera, and Paule de Brindes pining for her lost love, the narrator bids us his farewell, and takes his parting shot, with this remarkable declaration: "Don't we live fast after all, and doesn't the old order change? Don't say art isn't mighty! I shall give you some more illustrations of it yet" (*CO,* 431). Once again, and as always, the social categories of the "old order" and the esthetic categories of "art" are equally paralyzed by the ironist's apostrophe. But within the final avowal of further "illustrations"—itself equivocally blending references to the pictorial and the narrative arts—we may perhaps locate not a welcome promise, but merely a quiet threat.

III

By way of conclusion, we consider another complication in the task of determining "authorship." Along with a critical reading of this story, Adeline Tintner offers as a possible source for "Collaboration" the actual collaboration of Rudyard

Kipling and Wolcott Balestier on their novel *The Naulahka*. I do not wish to oppose her suggestion, which seems convincing enough, but I would like to point out what seem to be additional sources.

Matthiessen and Murdock, in their edition of The Notebooks,[6] concluded that "Collaboration" is one of the few tales not mentioned there; but as with "The Third Person" this seems not to be the case. On February 5, 1892, at about the time "Collaboration" would have been written, James made the following entry in his Notebooks:

> I was greatly struck, the other day, with something M. d'Estournelles, whom I met at Lady Brooke's, said to [me] about P.B.'s life and situation—in regard to his marriage, his prospects: that his only safety—*their* only safety, as a *ménage heureux,* resided in their remaining *loin de France*—abroad—far from Paris. From the moment they should return there their union would *have* to go to pieces—their safety as a *ménage heureux*—their mutual affection and cohesion. It was sad, but it was *comme ça*. Paris wouldn't *tolerate* a united pair; would inevitably and ruthlessly disintegrate it. When Lady B. said, 'C'est bien triste!,' the speaker said, 'Mon Dieu, madame, c'est comme ça!' Something probably to be done with the tragedy, the inevitable *fate,* of this; the prevision of it, on the part of a young couple, the mingled horror and fascination of the prospect. (*NB,* 63)

This reference to Paul Bourget (the "P.B." in question) and the circumstance of his marriage seems to mirror the condition of Félix Vendemer and Herman Heidenmauer at the end of "Collaboration," in their inevitable exile from Paris. In particular, the "mingled horror and fascination" serves as an accurate description of Vendemer's emotions.

Following directly upon this entry, James recorded a further anecdote: "Henry Adams spoke to me the other day of the end [of] certain histories of which, years ago, in London he had seen the beginning—poor Lady M.H., who broke off her engagement with X.Y.Z. on the eve of marriage and now trails about at the tail of her mother—or some other fine lady—a dreary old maid" (*NB*, 63). In itself this idea is barely developed, but coupled with the reference to Bourget above it could well be viewed as providing a model for Vendemer's beloved Paule de Brindes. As a story that hinges upon the notion of artistic creation, where the salons are filled with painters and poets, composers and novelists, "Collaboration" might well be seen as the product of some five novelists: along with Rudyard Kipling and Wolcott Balestier we could add the names Paul Bourget and Henry Adams, and, in passing, one Henry James.

Not Finishing "Hugh Merrow"

The promise of further "illustrations" made by the narrator at the end of "Collaboration" is one that is in turn picked up by James repeatedly in his career, both in its fulfillment in the production of other, further fictions, and in the insertion into those fictions of further such promises. A promise implies a continuation, and with it a projected future in which action is contemplated along the lines of intention. Thus it effectively defers, for the duration of its holding, the matter of conclusion. In other words, a promise may be made to be broken, but the act of breaking it must also occur at some future time, a time created by the promise itself.

By way of deferring my own conclusion, I turn here to a text that has not fulfilled its promise, that will always apparently exist sometime in the future: "Hugh Merrow." This "unfinished" story, revealed for the first time to most readers of James only within the past year, offers its own particular promise to be the site of a new flux of Jamesian criticism, while at the same time portending that such a criticism will be difficult to engender, in that "Hugh Merrow," if only by virtue of its unfinished state, refuses to conform to our expectations of a James text. Hence the question of our expectations may well come into clearer focus here, where they can't hide as well behind that text. "Hugh Merrow" offers us a familiar, indeed a much repeated Jamesian situation—a portrait painter, one Hugh Merrow, is approached in his studio by a young and handsome couple with the peculiar request that he paint for them the portrait of a child that they have never been able to have themselves. The fragment extant tells the story of their negotiations, ending with Merrow's agreement to attempt the project.

Since Merrow is an artist, and the outlines of his art are at question in this story, "Hugh Merrow" will be a fertile ground for the continuing discussion of James's investigation of the relation between art and the real, including questions of the "portrait" as representation, or as the metaphor of fiction in the creation of authorial space. The issue of the portrait and its theoretical implications for the fiction of James is one that has been much discussed recently, and has provided some of the most interesting and significant of recent James criticism.[1] To continue that discussion here, however, would extend beyond the scope of the present study, in part because it would necessitate the importation of works of James's clearly within the bounds of his canon. I will instead look at another related and perhaps coterminous issue, attempting to place "Hugh Merrow" within a context (and thereby perhaps finishing the text that is not "finished"), the context of other James fictions which I perceive to grow from the same essential beginning.

I propose then to examine here a small element of a series of fictions that is grouped together first on the basis of motif, that of the construction of an absent person through an artistic rendering, but also on the issue of where and how a text is to be delimited, and therefore "defined." What is the beginning and ending of a story, and where and how can we say that it begins and ends? The texts I have in mind are "Maud-Evelyn," "The Tone of Time" and "Hugh Merrow." What I seek to demonstrate in looking at these particular texts is that they are in effect all *one* text. Though permuted in several different directions, we have in these three not different stories, but the different workings out of the same relation, different takes on the same basic subject—as though an alternative is being proposed and then abandoned, or perhaps superseded by another. I should note here that Tzvetan Todorov has already seen the first two stories—"Maud-Evelyn" and "The Tone of Time"—as indicative of the same issue in James's short fiction (and we will return to Todorov's views later in this chapter). But while this may be so, what we seem to read are different stories, and this is the space that I seek to delimit here. It will involve the switching from a consideration of the portrait as function to that of the narrative modes and strategies employed in the construction of these texts, and the acts of distancing and deferral found therein. The result is that we will take for granted the central presence of the portrait, and look instead toward the portrait's frame—its design and shape, and the matter of whether that frame has been finished, and by whom.

I

What a glance at James's Notebooks reveals, in part, is how closely allied all these stories are, even what a muddle the now discrete strands that comprise them seem in their appearance there. It also reveals a virtual obsession with the subject, so that it is astounding that the execution of the stories is sufficiently different in each case as to clear James of the charge of gross repetitiveness. For well over five years, the notion of constructing human identity through an artistic rendering recurs in the anecdotes he recorded in the Notebooks. Paul Bourget contributed the notion of "imitation" and the loss of identity consequent on the assumption of it; from the instance of Dr. Henri Cazalis assuming a pen name James extrapolated a scenario where such an act would entail the gradual fading of the person's original identity; and from a story idea conceived by Luigi Gualdo and reported secondhand to

James was gained the conception of constructing the identity of a nonexistent child through a portrait.[2] This "Gualdo notion," as James himself was to term it, of the artistic construction of identity, emerges in three separate fictional executions of the same idea: the construction of a mate for a male in "Maud-Evelyn," one for a female in "The Tone of Time," and a child for a barren couple in "Hugh Merrow"—an entire family.[3] Though conceiving of this fictional direction as the constitution of an equally fictional family may lead naturally to a psychologistic approach to these stories, particularly one where James's personal psychology is labelled and utilized, I prefer instead to focus on their resemblances through formal similarities. For the moment, then, James stands as the Master in his role as the constructor of these fictions, and not as the well of loneliness and compensation that would be their source.

It bears repeating at this point that the "Gualdo notion" is one that encompasses all three of the stories we are viewing here, so that their appearance in the Notebooks reflects not just three growths from a single seed, but the overlapping of each presentation with every other. One entry in particular, that of May 7, 1898, points this out with some clarity:

> 8. Gualdo's story of the child *retournée*—the acquisition, construction (by portrait, etc. ???) of an ANCESTOR, instead of *l'Enfant*. The setting up of some one who must *have lived: un vrai mort*. . . .
>
> 9. (In same key.) The woman who wants to have *been* married—to *have become a widow*. *She* may come, *à la Gualdo*, to the painter to have the portrait painted—the portrait of her husband. (*NB, 169*)

We can see here that the original idea (bearing the pun for a moment) of the *child* constructed by the portrait is shifted onto one who has come "before" in the entry designated as number eight: the rest of this note will sketch out the design of "Maud-Evelyn." Number nine, on the other hand, shifts the burden onto a "husband." In both cases, the source is the "Gualdo notion," as James clearly indicates by reference to that name, by the notation of writing a different story in the "same key," and by the italicization of what seems to be conceived of here as the crucial element, expressed in the perfect tense. And in both cases, the original and generative notion regarding the child pertains, the same "Gualdo notion" that is to form the basis of "Hugh Merrow." The mixing of these narratives is brought home again by an entry on February 16 of the next year, when he states: "I pick up for a minute the idea of the portrait *à la* Gualdo—it haunts me: oh, what things, what *swarms* haunt me!" (*NB, 179*). Here we see not only the persistence of this theme, but also the way that it is pluralized almost as soon as it is enunciated: one "idea" quickly becomes "swarms."

One further item from the Notebooks deserves mention in passing: James refers to the "Gualdo notion" twice more, on September 11, 1900, and June 12, 1901. Since "Maud-Evelyn" was published in April of 1900 and "The Tone of

Time" in November of that same year, these entries would seem to indicate that the treatment of this subject had not yet been exhausted, and that he planned to return to it. The recapitulation of this idea would come to form the fragment of "Hugh Merrow," and thus we can assume that the composition of that piece dates from approximately this time, or at least that the decision to suspend work on it (if such a decision was in fact made) comes only after mid-1901. But if the date of composition is difficult to place, it is no more so than the text of "Hugh Merrow" itself. That is our next task, and in order to do so it is necessary to articulate the borders of the space that surrounds it, in "Maud-Evelyn" and "The Tone of Time."

II

In "The Tone of Time," the first person narrator, himself a painter of portraits, reports on the request made of him by one Mrs. Bridgenorth to paint the portrait of a husband she has never had. He is immediately though dimly aware of the strange circumstance surrounding this request, and curious about its source, but recognizes also that he is incapable of entering into it. The narrator notes at the beginning of the story that his participation in a collaborative production is impossible, when he tells us that "My trick won't serve for this."[4] Instead, he passes off the assignment to a friend, Mary Tredick, whose style is more in keeping with the requirements of the commission—she is better able to provide the "tone of time" necessary to the picture. The tale goes on to sketch the startling coincidence of these two women's histories, and the blossoming of a long dead passion into a renewed quest for revenge.

The machinery of competition between the women is interesting enough in its own right, and forms the greater part of the story, but I am more interested here in the borders that enclose the space where it occurs, and that mark it off for our inspection. "The Tone of Time" is "framed," in the sense that its narrator is involved in the plot only as an intermediary, observer and reporter. The creation of the portrait, and through it the fiction, of their shared dead lover belongs to the women; they sustain it and produce it, and their collaboration in that project is extreme, even though they never meet. The narrator's part in this is such that he can only report, and from some distance, the emptiness that belongs in the common past of these two women. Thus we have here a kind of funneling of perspective, best expressed in the exit from the story in the last paragraph. By this time the principals have both died, and the narrator has only the representation left, from which or with which to construct his own narrative fiction, that of the story we read:

> But it was the end of my vision. I could only write, ruefully enough, to Mrs Bridgenorth, whom I never met again, but of whose death—preceding by a couple of years Mary Tredick's—I happened to hear. This is an old man's tale. I have inherited the picture, in the deep beauty of which, however, darkness still lurks. No one, strange to say, has ever recognised the model, but everyone asks his name. I don't even know it. (*TT*, 214)

The distance between the "real" and the representation of the real postulated by this text is maintained in its conclusion. While the portrait mediates between the absent man and the women who loved him, this narrator, and especially the conclusion of his narration, mediates between us and the strange unexplained holes in the histories of its characters. Though we see the composition of the portrait in "The Tone of Time" (where we don't in "Hugh Merrow"), that portrait takes on its significance only through a layered process of actions, from transmission of the original idea to its execution to its investment with significance, and a variety of wrong turns, principally by the narrator, along that way. At the completion of the story, the fiction is put together, but only in the recognition that loose ends still remain. The process of fiction-making continues, in the requests for a name and a history of the subject, questions the answers to which are not forthcoming.

Leon Edel has called "Maud-Evelyn" an "unpleasant story," and I think that most readers would agree with him.[5] It relates the history of its central character, Marmaduke, who in rebounding from being rejected by his desired Lavinia, falls in love with the long dead Maud-Evelyn, and who, on the promptings of her worshipful parents the Dedricks, gradually convinces himself that he was once married to her. An obsession with the dead is perhaps seen more clearly here than in any James story other than the "ghost" stories, except of course for "The Altar of the Dead." One of the curious things about "Maud-Evelyn" in fact is that it seems to be almost the same story as "The Altar of the Dead," with a reversal of affect—where we can find a macabre flavor to the latter, it simply doesn't have the same "unpleasantness" as the former, though the reason for this is obscure. Is it merely because Stransom's loss is of "real" people, who had really lived and been lost, while Marmaduke is engaged in the construction of someone he never knew? If so, the artist's construction of personality would be exposed in these tales as something less than an expression of genuine feeling; rather, it would appear to be the substitute for an inability, which amounts to a refusal, to enter "life." But if, in "The Altar of the Dead," death as the site on which communion is placed becomes tolerable, if slightly grotesque, the same judgment ought not hold for "Maud-Evelyn," because there is no such altar here, nor the attempt to erect one. These two stories share the superficial resemblance of being "about" the dead, but the focus of "Maud-Evelyn" is on the act of construction that takes place "around" this absence. The channel in these fictions is one of producing a narrative that will serve to enclose the dead—and we see here the connection to Minny Temple, Milly Theale, Flora Saunt, and other instances—for here, in these stories, James plays with the possible permutations of narrative art as a deflection and container of those who are lost.

Similar to its employment in "The Tone of Time," the use of a narrative frame acts as one such deflection in "Maud-Evelyn." In fact, "Maud-Evelyn" begins with the distance of the frame by lodging the story in an old woman, and giving a rich description of her:

> Old Lady Emma, who for a while had said nothing, scarcely even appearing to listen and letting the chatter, which was indeed plainly beside the mark, subside of itself, came back from a mental absence to observe that if what had happened to Lavinia was wonderful, certainly, what had for years gone before it, led up to it, had likewise not been without some singular features. From this we perceived that Lady Emma had a story—a story moreover out of the ken even of those of her listeners acquainted with the quiet person who was the subject of it. . . . Lady Emma, who always reminded me of a fine old instrument that has first to be tuned, agreed, after a few of our scrapings and fingerings, that, having said so much, she couldn't, without wantonly tormenting us, forbear to say all.[6]

The details of this introduction drive home the significance of Lady Emma as the storyteller: she gains the deference of her age, her reputation as a storyteller is familiarly, even teasingly portrayed, and her subsequent speech is clearly marked off from the "chatter" that precedes it. We are informed, in short, that the utterance to follow has import, and that it comes from a distinctive speaker. But the interesting and easily overlooked aspect of this beginning is not Lady Emma, but the presence of the second narrator, that unnamed presumably male member of the party who is essentially continuous with James himself, and who tells us the story of Lady Emma's story. This narrative technique provides distance from the issue at hand, and in lodging the narrative with a female, and an old one, it carries along with it a certain perspective that is patently different from the narrator's. The story we read here, usually remembered as Lady Emma's story, is therefore itself all given within quotation marks—and it is at this juncture that we must question whether that story is distinct from the "chatter" that precedes it by virtue of its being more "important," more "true," or merely more "constructed."

The story told by Lady Emma is itself enclosed in a story told by the narrator, and Lady Emma tells not just a story, but a story *about* a story, the fiction-making that is Marmaduke's (and to some extent Lavinia's) *raison d'être*. This distancing seems somehow necessary, and explains as well the absence of the Dedricks—why they, as prime creators of the myth, must be absent. Their primary authorship of the myth of Maud-Evelyn is presumed, but we are never made privy to it, or to them. As Tzvetan Todorov has perceived, "the Jamesian narrative is always based on the quest for an absolute and absent cause."[7] Note in this regard the way in which Lady Emma steadfastly refuses to meet them, only having in passing a glimpse of them, and how this isolation and boundary drawing is supported by her notions of social caste. In making the Dedricks untouchable, Lady Emma is able to construct her fiction about them and Marmaduke without the interference of troublesome facts.

That is to say, in part what we have in "Maud-Evelyn" is a telescoping series of fictions, each one constructed by a different character in the story (or out of it?), each one containing the others. The chain of fictions runs on a continuum, stretching from us as readers at one end to Maud-Evelyn at the other: the readers—Henry James—the unnamed male narrator—Lady Emma/Lavinia/

Marmaduke (with overlaps here)—the Dedricks—the dead daughter, Maud-Evelyn. This story does indeed posit death as an unknowable absent center, and further, we have different degrees of that absence, running from "most dead" to "least dead," in reverse order of the chain above: Maud-Evelyn, who is already and always dead—the Dedricks, who die in succession—Marmaduke, who follows them near the end of the story—Lavinia, the inheritor of relics, an old maid and "widow"—Lady Emma, herself old. Tzvetan Todorov has indeed pointed out that death functions as the absent and motivating center of these narratives, and I take my cue from him here, but while Todorov sees essentially one absence at the center of this text, towards which the separate characters embody different attitudes, like the spokes of a wheel, I would see the narrative structure here as a series of increasingly large concentric circles, like the sections of a collapsible telescope, each cylinder enclosing the other. Such a structure would offer a new wrinkle on the term "circumscription"—each "life" is in fact "written around" every other. The schematic distinction thus proposed is a crucial one, for by the end of the story Maud-Evelyn is increasingly distant and finally disappears, replaced by other deaths, other absences. And this may indicate something not so much about life as about a fiction's interrelation with that life: that that continuum of fictionalization may be open-ended, and we presume an end only because we are ourselves at one "end," in the fiction of identity that we construct for ourselves. It may well be that, in "Maud-Evelyn," death serves not so much as absent center, but as a horizon point beyond which we cannot see, because of the provisional closings, always being redrawn, around our circle of narrative.

This may explain too the inability to judge whether the situation at the center of "Maud-Evelyn" is acceptable or not. Each of the characters is involved in the authorship of a fiction that essentially includes all the others, and for this to go on the maintenance of distance must pertain. That is, Lady Emma's fiction of a happy marriage, Lavinia's happy fiction of Marmaduke never marrying another (conflicting with Lady Emma's), Marmaduke's fiction of a wife (conflicting with Lavinia's), the Dedricks' primary fiction—each contains, absorbs, and overlaps the others. While we as readers have at least the momentary opportunity to see that they function as competition, we are still also as readers caught in the same cycle of expectation and construction and relation. One can speak here of the connection of portraiture to narrative arts, in the way that the latter can freeze the portrait of the other in a place where it cannot move, but we must note that in "Maud-Evelyn" we can see that such a freezing is not without dangers, and certainly that it is not without sacrifices—not only of another contemplated life, which is after all only another fiction, but in the energy of perpetual motion and interpretation needed to sustain that fiction.

The conclusion of "Maud-Evelyn" poses one further example of that energy. Lavinia's inheritance of the fine "things" Marmaduke bought for Maud-Evelyn comes only after they can be successfully incorporated into her fiction with the help of Lady Emma, a conversion that is almost ontological in nature. Formerly, the things "belonged" to the dead girl, but the death of Marmaduke and the absence of other players leaves them reassignable in terms of significance: Marmaduke's fiction dies with him, while Lavinia's fiction is opened up and made vital by the importation of "Marmaduke," now at last in the place she always wanted him, never to marry another. Now, since the things belong to Marmaduke and he to her, ownership is not just transferable but desirable, and this is why she is spoken of as having a "piece of luck" in the story's first paragraph. As well, the implicit suggestion of the value of the old things, and the inheritance of the Dedricks' money through Marmaduke to Lavinia—this is what Lady Emma had been after all along, in the provision of a fortune for her beloved charge, one of nine children, self-reliant but alone. It is as though death opens the possibility of finishing a differing conglomerate of fortune, and while the focus on money may well provoke distaste and an accusation of crass morbidity, it should be remembered that the "value" of the things functions much the same way as the Dedricks' social position, as the indicator of constructed circles of relation and narration, a construction that is never quite finished. As Lady Emma says of these things at the end of her story, "Tell *you* about them, you say? My dear man, everything" (*ME*, 75). Here, the cycle of fiction-construction is explicitly promised a continuance, which is what it gets from James, and from us, in the willing participation in the writing of yet another story to circumscribe it.

III

"Hugh Merrow" has about it the air of abandonment. Judging from the repeated Notebook references to the story's idea, the "Gualdo" notion, it would appear that that idea is taken up here in its fullest form, that of dealing directly with the creation of a "child," and then left off at the end of the first section—a promising notion abandoned, and for reasons that will no doubt remain obscure. The very short history of its criticism, however, threatens already the subsumption of this text under the ensign of the Master,[8] despite troubling questions that it poses for exactly that approach. The dissemination of this text only after a full 50 years had passed since its discovery, despite the prior emergence of practically everything written by the Master, brings to the fore a complex of questions regarding the sociology of proprietary interest involved in the construction of *oeuvre*. Further, the realization that this text somehow survived the celebrated burning of manuscripts by James (the burning took place in the autumn of 1909, perhaps a half-dozen years after the composition of "Hugh Merrow") would seem to open questions of the Master's own stance with respect to this "fragment."[9] But whether "Hugh Merrow" has suffered suppression, by James or by his readers—perhaps as an embarrassment, as unfinished, as a repetition of "The Liar" and especially "The Real Thing" in setting and situation, as an incipient plagiarism of Gualdo's idea—it would seem that Lyall H. Powers's suggestion is a good one: since it is "rather an anomaly, it seems to require a special category."[10]

"Hugh Merrow" is a unique Jamesian text in its relationship to authorship: given the historical "facts," the relation of this story to the rest of his fiction is unexplained. Not published, not spoken to, not recorded in the Notebooks as a separate entity distinct from other executions—and especially in its appearance only now—this text seems to necessitate the comparison of it to the body of James's work that we know. In other words, the exposure of the unfinished work to the light will necessitate the manipulation of the newcomer to fit already established parameters—even though there is a strangeness here that doesn't go away. The effect of this critically is that in a curious way it keeps the writer as both alive *and* dead. That is, the emergence of new work makes it seem as if that work was just produced, providing a new opportunity to read a new text by Henry James—but "James" is so closed off and controlled that that text cannot be read as anything other than an example of that critical construct. Even if "Hugh Merrow" presents something different, it must be absorbed into the already established framework of ideas surrounding a series of James texts, in this case the text of the Master, which is so complicated and nuanced as to supply the causal force of its own prolongation. If we try to look instead at the text of "Hugh Merrow" itself, what do we find?

First, the notion that this story is unfinished comes from a view that sees it as a kind of conditional—that is, the plot of "Hugh Merrow" is seen as, "if the artist paints the portrait, what will happen?" This is certainly the outline of the situation in "The Liar," "The Tone of Time," and "The Real Thing"—but what if this is the wrong question? What if the question of "Hugh Merrow" is instead, "if the artist *agrees* to paint the portrait, what will happen?" In this case, we have a completed plot. In other words, the crux of "Hugh Merrow" would seem to lie around the story of negotiations, making the actual commission of the portrait nothing more than a pretext for those negotiations, and if this is the case, there is no place else to go because we have been there already. This doesn't mean that "Hugh Merrow" is not dissatisfying—it is—but it does point out that our expectations can be so strong as to preclude certain kinds of responses. The "text" of "Hugh Merrow" is thus difficult to locate, since it stands in a compelling intertextual relationship with other Jamesian works. We might possibly see this story standing by itself, *if* it were of another time and place, *if* it were under another author's signature, or *if* it is viewed as the marker of Henry James as a kind of ultramodern minimalist. But given the wider text of Henry James as we have constituted him, there is recourse only to the Master.

A few of these intertextual connections require specific tracing. Note first that the story of the negotiations for the portrait is more fully recounted here than elsewhere. James omits the first meeting from "The Tone of Time," even though it is proposed in the story's outline in the Notebooks. By omitting what is known, by not saying all that it would be possible to say, in "The Tone of Time," James reserves a place in which there is something to say later. In "The Liar" and "The Real Thing," on the other hand, we find that the issue of artistic rendering becomes the reflector of sensibility—with the creations there indicative of the personalities of the artists—and the theoretical mirror of narrative. But in "Hugh Merrow," since we don't get to that point, if we were ever intended to, the story takes a different tack, though under the same guise. Thus we must either understand the relation of the characters through a postulated later treatment that would show their "true" relation, no doubt in keeping with our expectations of James, or we can infer that relation from what is before us.

Other connections obtain as well. The egotism of the artist that inheres in the central characters in "The Real Thing" and especially "The Liar" reappears here: Hugh Merrow is one who "saw it all, at any rate—and partly from habit, for he had been approached repeatedly for a like purpose, such being the penalty of a signal gift. . . ."[11] But the most striking linkage is in the repetition of a sexual tension between the painter and the woman before him. In "The Tone of Time," James invites his reader to infer things about its narrator through the teasing references he makes to an intimacy between him and Mary Tredick, that he might too be a love interest, but this association is broken off, perhaps because Mary Tredick is herself a painter. The attraction between Merrow and Mrs. Archdean, however, is apparent, and carried throughout the fragment, resembling that between the narrator and Mrs. Capadose in "The Liar." Instead of Merrow considering the effect of his assignment per se, we find him "thinking that she was ever so delicately and dimly pretty, that her mouth was as sweet as her eyes, and her nose as handsome as her hair; and he was thinking other things besides" (*HM*, 591).

What those "other things" may have been we can only presume, but we learn with some speed that Merrow's feeling for Mrs. Archdean, and her request for the portrait of her nonexistent child, are quickly to collide with a sense of pervasive death. In fact, the place that Merrow joins her is exactly that of death: in his spying on her reaction to his painting at their previous contact, he hears " 'Oh, it kills me!' —that was what she had strangely sighed; yet without turning off and rather as if she liked to be killed. Merrow had himself turned off—he had got rather more than he wanted" (*HM*, 590). The conjunction here, through the operative mode of euphemism, is now complete: the "other things" of Merrow is joined by Mrs. Archdean liking to be "killed." But the "deadness" in "Hugh Merrow" emerges elsewhere as well, when James tells us that he had returned to his painting in the exhibit "partly for the joy of again seeing himself so luckily hung" (*HM*, 590). The identification of the painter with his work so thoroughly is of course striking, but again we have the metaphor and the pun, of being "hung," as a kind of flash point: how much is the collision of one's productions with one's self—and the creation of identity found there—contiguous with a kind of (desirable) death? The answer is not forthcoming, especially in that Merrow's response to the Archdeans is one of being "moved," but not as a painter: rather, "It was as if something might come to him if he did consent, though what might come indeed might not be a thing that he himself should call a picture" (*HM*, 595).

A comparison of the narrative modes of "Hugh Merrow" with those of its closest relatives is also revealing. "Maud-Evelyn" is a first person narrative, deflected by the frame around Lady Emma's story. "The Tone of Time" is also in the first person, distanced by the external quality of its narrator being merely an intermediary to the arrangement. "Hugh Merrow," conversely, is in the third person, and thus presumably more distant—but this is exactly the opposite of the case. In a first-person narration, we construct a fiction of the author's voice that is one step removed from that author—it is after all a character who does the speaking, who is the "I" there. But in "Hugh Merrow," the narrative mode of the third person puts in the author's hands a greater closeness to the event, and a greater demand for control. Less responsibility for the perception of the character, for the truth of his utterance, is given to the character himself, while more of this is retained by the Master. In that sense it is more the place where we find the Master with all his mastery at stake.

We near here the point of Cynthia Ozick's suggestions, and in the temptation to psychologize the author into the character say that James sees too much of himself threatening to become evident in "Hugh Merrow" for comfort, and therefore he drops away from it, in haste, for self-protection. If one is so inclined, one can view the use of the painter's medium as a covert expression of James's inability to express his sexuality, since the latter is viewed as the more taboo—for us, maybe. But what if the reverse is true: that what is being exposed in "Hugh Merrow" is the cloak which conceals the artist, the curtain behind which he constructs his illusions. The moment of that nakedness is fearful indeed, for the Master, and if one thinks to engage in it, one contemplates an act clearly criminal. Might it not be the case then that that outlaw status is already existent in the composition of "Hugh Merrow," and that the sublimation of it is *into* the sexual, not in fact the other way around? Thus we would see why, as Mrs. Capadose has her Colonel and Mrs. Monarch has her Major, it is necessary that Mrs. Archdean have her Captain. All are titles of rank and authority, officers in service of the established order, and powerful inhibiting presences. It is an inhibition perhaps almost necessary, as compensation both for what has already been contemplated and fulfilled, and for what is to come:

> "And about what will be the age——?"
> "Well, say about eight."
> This made them at once eager. "Then you'll readily try?" They spoke in the same breath.
> "I'll try my very hardest!"
> They looked at each other in joy, too grateful even to speak. It was wonderful how he pleased them, and he felt that he liked it. If he could only keep it up! (*HM*, 596)

This, the ending of "Hugh Merrow," closes the encounter with a further promise of continuance, and thus ends the narrative with a kind of circular closure, a circumscription that leads us not outward, but back inward to the first paragraph of the story.

IV

It was only for a moment that Merrow failed to place them, aware as he was, as soon as they were introduced, of having already seen them. That was all they at first showed, except that they were shy, agitated, almost frightened: they had been present to him, and within a few days, though unwittingly, in some connection that had made them interesting. He had recovered the connection even before the lady spoke—spoke, he could see, out of the depths of their diffidence, and making the effort, he could also see, that the woman, in the delicate case, is always left by the man to make.

James, "Hugh Merrow"

If we examine this paragraph under the critical microscope, we discover several interesting features lying in its structural arrangement. Picking up at the end of the first independent clause, at "aware as he was," we find ourselves confronted with four conclusions that come in rapid succession: first, the "awareness" of Merrow, previously acquired and encompassing all that is to follow; second, the notion of "introduction" as an encapsulation of complexity into the simplicity of rubric; third, Merrow's "having already seen" acting as a further encapsulation, this time in the visual medium; and fourth, the extension of this visual medium into the concrete detail of description—shyness, agitation, fright—making the Archdeans "present," realized in qualities that draw in the perceiver and make him fasten on what is in them (which has been constructed by *him*) that is "interesting." What we have been describing here are the methods and functions of the *artist*, whether visual or fictional—the previously held genres, the squaring off of field, the attention to medium and execution of particulars. At this point, "Hugh Merrow" is effectively over, having told us that the artist is one who will connect the threads of experience into a coherency of definition, who will take the advent of outside material and form it into a whole. The figural moment of "Hugh Merrow," of all these fictions, is therefore the moment of composition, and what we as readers see and concentrate on is merely its after-effects, which is all that we have noted so far.

I have traced previously this notion of a determinative first paragraph with respect to "Glasses," and offer the observation that much the same is true with "Hugh Merrow." One further example may be useful, to illustrate the recurrence of these structures in James's short fictions. The beginning of "The Real Thing" is as follows:

When the porter's wife (she used to answer the house-bell) announced "A gentleman—with a lady, sir," I had, as I often had in those days, for the wish was father to the thought, an immediate vision of sitters. Sitters my visitors in this case proved to be; but not in the sense I should have preferred. However, there was nothing at first to indicate that they might not have come for a portrait. The gentleman, a man of fifty, very high and very straight, with a moustache.[12]

Practically every separable strain of "The Real Thing" is to be found in this portion of the first paragraph: the "porter's wife" imports the distinction of social class to figure so prominently later; the announcement and "immediate vision" relay the painter's craft; the cliché of "the wish is father to the thought" is especially pregnant with regard to the subsequent drama of realistic portrayal; the distinction of sitters and "sitters" foreshadows the later contest of types, and emphasizes as well the dilemma of a "mistaken" vision; and the artist/narrator, unable to paint them later, will "paint" them now, verbally.

Both here and in "Hugh Merrow," we as readers see only the traces of effect, the consequences from that original moment of creation of the image—like a fictional big bang, followed by, and presumably causing, the observable explosive residue it leaves behind. But the presumption of the initial creative explosion is always only that, a presumption, basing its authority on an imposition of structure from the outside onto an absence that sets it moving. After this, the decision of how many traces to follow is essentially ours, as long as the fiction allows the continued tracing of traces, as long as a promise is given, so that closure remains an illusion and the fragility of the fiction is preserved.[13] "Hugh Merrow" offers this, in the promise to so compose the painting of the absent child, and from here all considerations of the usage of representation in James's fictions can flow. What we need to see is the point from which they spring—really a "point" now, a presumption of geometric location that is itself empty, and that point is found in the initial phrase of "Hugh Merrow"—"it was only for a moment." The genesis of "Hugh Merrow," and of the rest of these fictions, is that point not filled, an emptiness to be construed later. As an emptiness, it is inscribed only in a flash, and cannot be grasped by definitions, as they are merely substitutes for the moment. These substitutes then act as deferrals of the facing of that moment too directly and for too long. There is also, in a sense, a tremendous loneliness here, in the recognition that the moment of speech only emphasizes a lack at the very instant of filling it. But the prospect of not doing so, of not reading and not constructing, is even more disquieting.

All three of the fictions we are considering here have their own sense of closure, and of the options involved therein; and in two cases, that closure is one that itself, paradoxically, insures an opening. That is, "Maud-Evelyn" has closure by opening in that the story stops at the completion of one fiction(s), that of Marmaduke/Lavinia, but insures as well the perpetuation of others—Lady Emma's, the narrator's, James's and ours. In "The Tone of Time," the fiction stops with the deaths of the participants, and opens with the persistence of the painting that itself provokes the necessity of understanding it, not just in the narrator but in all spectators of the portrait, including James and us. "Hugh Merrow," however, is the oddity, in that this story provides a full closure, in the agreement to do the painting. Once the agreement is made, the task taken up, all is done—the beginning carries with it its own ending.

Todorov mentions that narrative deferral is necessary, because the omniscient narrator is able to see the absence, and to communicate it, and if he does that, the narrative will collapse. Thus, the secret at the center must be deflected and hidden, and the main mode of so doing is to locate the narration in a character far enough away from it physically, temporally and experientially to maintain the construction of fiction. James's choice of the omniscient narrator for "Hugh Merrow" is then in effect an inability to carry on with the project of inscribing an absence at the center of things, or maybe, conversely, an abandonment, if only for the moment, of the recurrent use of this technique of absent centers. Since this abandonment takes place at the very beginning of "Hugh Merrow," and effectively requires it to be no more than a beginning, it is worth noting that while any beginning authorizes what proceeds from it, it also cuts out certain options as inconsonant if not impossible to transpire from the structure of that beginning. Still, the decision that proceeding is impossible would have to come from elsewhere: as Edward Said has said, in the undertaking of any beginning "there must be the desire, the will, and the true freedom to reverse oneself, to accept thereby the risks of rupture and discontinuity."[14] Has James found it impossible to accept that risk, or has he lacked the "true" freedom to do so? That is to say, if James's fictional being depends upon the Master's persona, an abandonment of that persona would mean that the absence at the center of these texts would not only be somehow impossibly present, but that it would grow to cover him, and that he too, as Master, would become absent, so that the framework of the house of fiction would come crashing down. As Said has indicated, in a comment especially pertinent to the case of "Hugh Merrow," "Stretching from start to finish is a fillable space, or time, pretty much there but, like a foundling, awaiting an author or a speaker to father it, to authorize its being."[15] If "Hugh Merrow" is therefore a beginning that negates its own ending, so that the agreement to paint the painting and reveal the absence is an agreement not to paint any paintings, or author any fictions, we have here a space that cannot be filled. The marking off of that space, paradoxically, prevents its filling, so that what we have can never even properly be called a beginning, but only a wrong move.

V

It may be a mistake to describe the action of "Maud-Evelyn" as the conflict between a series of fictionists. Maybe we would be more accurate in saying instead that the text breaks the boundaries between critic and fictionist, or at least assails those boundaries with unanswerable questions. After all, the critic also absorbs the text he grabs, dragging it into his discourse, in the production of his own competing text that would construe the original work and invest it with "meaning." Again, Edward Said: "A literary critic, for example, who is fastened on a text is a critic who, in demonstrating his right to speak, makes the text something that is continuous with his own discourse."[16] In that sense we could just as well say that James's seeming inability to move in a different direction is not just a flight, since it has the effect of preserving a career and the texts formerly produced there. But here again we face the issue of the consistency that grounds the canon, in transforming a retreat into a strategic maneuver.

On his deathbed, in the midst of disjointed ramblings, complaints about his throat and letters to his family signed "Napoléone," Henry James dictated the following remarkably coherent paragraph:

> These final and faded remarks all have some interest and some character—but this should be extracted by a highly competent person only—some such, whom I don't presume to name, will furnish last offices. In fact I do without names not wish to exaggerate the defect of their absence. Invoke more than one kind presence, several could help, and many would—but it is all better too much left than too much done. (*NB*, 584)

This invocation opens the way for subsequent readers, in an expression both of a need for those readers and a resentment of them—that succession of speaking voices that would challenge the Master and through those challenges help him to survive, and persist. If so, does that mean for example that the frame around "Hugh Merrow" is unfinished, open? For who to enter, for who to escape? The answer is elusive, but whether or not "Hugh Merrow" ends or begins, Henry James looks to the endless opening of readings, one of which is here.

Or perhaps "Hugh Merrow" is in fact finished, accomplishing all that it intends to do, in following out the option that it sets up. What then is the reason for its not being published or spoken of? Because it conflicts so profoundly with the expectations of James's readers—including ours? To offer "Hugh Merrow" as a text by Henry James is to strike against all the conventions of plot that inform James's fiction—it is a text that is not in that sense "masterly." But that does not mean that it is not finished, or that it is not "finished" enough; and thus we can understand why it survived the burning of the manuscripts, in that, unlike other notes, this has the value of being still useful, needing to be preserved in its only version.

Or perhaps this does not finish the matter. To do so, to presume to finish "Hugh Merrow," is to engage in but another act of critical perspectivism, existing on a continuum of criticism that does not and cannot end. Even as we speak to "Hugh Merrow," in the presumptuous act of calling it rounded off, we open it up and deny the closure that James recognized and provided there. Instead, we would do better to recognize our place, as "kind presences" that are always "absent."

Or perhaps another perspective, from a reading not yet articulated, is required.

Notes

Chapter 1

1. Frank Kermode, *Forms of Attention* (Chicago: University of Chicago Press, 1985), 62.

2. Michel Foucault, "The Discourse on Language," in *The Archaeology of Knowledge,* trans. A. M. Sheridan Smith (New York: Random House, 1972), 216.

3. For two revealing discussions of the literary canon as repository of "value," see Barbara Herrnstein Smith, "Contingencies of Value," and Charles Altieri, "An Idea and Ideal of a Literary Canon," in *Canons,* ed. Robert von Hallberg (Chicago: University of Chicago Press, 1984). These essays originally appeared in *Critical Inquiry* 10 (1983).

4. Foucault, "Discourse on Language," 222.

5. Ross Chambers, *Story and Situation: Narrative Seduction and the Power of Fiction* (Minneapolis: University of Minnesota Press, 1984), chapter 7.

6. Ibid., 165.

7. Leon Edel and Lyall H. Powers, eds., *The Complete Notebooks of Henry James* (New York: Oxford University Press, 1987), 187, 118. Subsequent references given parenthetically as *NB.*

8. Chambers, *Story and Situation,* 160–61.

9. The nature of the absence at the center of "The Figure in the Carpet" has already been persuasively examined by Tzvetan Todorov, in the context of a wider discussion of the theory of narrativity. See *The Poetics of Prose,* trans. Richard Howard (Ithaca, NY: Cornell University Press, 1977), especially chapter 10.

10. Chambers, *Story and Situation,* 155.

11. Ibid., 168.

12. See Gilles Deleuze and Felix Guattari, *Kafka: Toward a Minor Literature,* trans. Dana Polan (Minneapolis: University of Minnesota Press, 1986); and Louis A. Renza, *"A White Heron" and the Question of Minor Literature* (Madison: University of Wisconsin Press, 1984).

13. Deleuze and Guattari, *Kafka,* 17.

14. Rowe in particular has met the problem of the "Master" square on, in chapter 1 of *The Theoretical Dimensions of Henry James* (Madison: University of Wisconsin Press, 1984), and my discussion

here takes several cues from his work. See also Susanne Kappeler, *Writing and Reading in Henry James* (London: Macmillan, 1980), and Allon White, *The Uses of Obscurity: The Fiction of Early Modernism* (London: Routledge and Kegan Paul, 1981).

15. For a precise and outspoken discussion of the institutional implications of canon mongering, see Terry Eagleton's *Literary Theory: An Introduction* (Minneapolis: University of Minnesota Press, 1983), especially chapter 6.

16. Kermode, *Forms of Attention,* 74.

Chapter 2

1. Henry James, *The Art of the Novel: Critical Prefaces by Henry James,* ed. R. P. Blackmur (New York: Scribner's, 1934), 213. Subsequent references given parenthetically as *AN.*

2. Perhaps the most important work on this story is that of James Kraft, who points out the "multifarious" quality of the letters with regard to James's investigations of the notion of point of view. But Kraft too cannot resist a potshot at "A Bundle of Letters" when he says that "the situation is too clever to be serious." See James Kraft, *The Early Tales of Henry James* (Carbondale, IL: Southern Illinois University Press, 1969), 110–16.

3. Tony Tanner, "James's Little Tarts," *The Spectator,* Jan. 4, 1963, p. 19.

4. Cornelia Pulsifer Kelley, *The Early Development of Henry James,* rev. ed. (Urbana, IL: University of Illinois Press, 1965), 273.

5. Kelley notes that this story has no "plot," that "nothing happens in the way of real complications," in *Early Development,* 274. Granville H. Jones, in turn, states that "A Bundle of Letters" is of "inconsequential effect": see *Henry James's Psychology of Experience* (The Hague: Mouton, 1975), 59. The idea that nothing happens—a curious indictment for most works of fiction—becomes curiouser still when applied to James, for whom little ever "happens," in the conventional sense.

6. Leon Edel, Introduction to vol. 4, *The Complete Tales of Henry James,* ed. Leon Edel (Philadelphia: Lippincott, 1962), 7.

7. Robert Adams Day, *Told in Letters: Epistolary Fiction before Richardson* (Ann Arbor: University of Michigan Press, 1966), 7.

8. Henry James, "A Bundle of Letters," in Leon Edel, ed., *The Complete Tales of Henry James,* vol. 4 (Philadelphia: Lippincott, 1962), 427. Subsequent references given parenthetically as *BL.*

9. Roland Barthes, *A Lover's Discourse,* trans. Richard Howard (New York: Hill and Wang, 1978), 152.

10. Ibid.

11. Ibid., 154.

12. In his short fiction, James demanded of himself the precision and terseness rarely found in his novels. This interchange is readily familiar to James readers as the distillation of some one hundred pages of *The American.*

13. Miranda can as well be likened to the Miranda of *The Tempest,* a fellow *naïve* who heralds the promise of a "brave new world." More interesting, though, is the role of Shakespeare's Miranda as a teacher of language:

> *Miranda.*   When thou didst not, savage,
> Know thine own meaning, but wouldst gabble like
> A thing most brutish, I endowed thy purposes
> With words that made them known. . . .
> *Caliban.* You taught me language, and my profit on't
> Is, I know how to curse. The red plague rid you
> For learning me your language!

(The Tempest, 1.2.355–64.)

14. My capsule formulation of the project of humor is indebted to the work of Neil Schmitz, particularly in chapter 1 of his *Of Huck and Alice: Humorous Writing in American Literature* (Minneapolis: University of Minnesota Press, 1983).

15. A penetrating analysis of the mechanisms of social control inscribed in the Jamesian text is found in Mark Seltzer's *Henry James and the Art of Power* (Ithaca: Cornell University Press, 1984). Seltzer notes that James's fiction "proclaims its outlawry even as the novel reproduces and promotes social systems of legality, supervision, and regulation. The novel secures and extends the very movements of power it ostensibly abjures" (p. 18).

16. White, *Uses of Obscurity,* 138.

Chapter 3

1. See Jones, *James's Psychology,* 62–63; and Adeline Tintner, "Poe's 'The Spectacles' and James' 'Glasses,'" *Poe Studies* 9 (1976): 53–54.

2. Wayne Booth, *The Rhetoric of Fiction* (Chicago: University of Chicago Press, 1961), 344.

3. Henry James, "Glasses," in Leon Edel, ed., *The Complete Tales of Henry James,* vol. 9 (Philadelphia: Lippincott, 1964), 322. Subsequent references given parenthetically as *GL.*

4. Sharon Dean, "The Myopic Narrator in Henry James's 'Glasses,'" *The Henry James Review* 4 (1983): 191–95.

5. Leon Edel, *Henry James: The Treacherous Years, 1895–1901* (New York: Lippincott, 1969), 83.

6. See Edel, *Henry James: The Treacherous Years,* 108–15.

7. Ibid., 113.

8. Quoted in Leon Edel, *Henry James: The Untried Years, 1843–1870* (New York: Lippincott, 1953), 331.

9. Ibid., 325.

10. It has been necessary to return to Matthiessen and Murdock's edition of *The Notebooks of Henry James* (New York: Oxford University Press, 1947) as the source of this quotation, since Edel and Powers's 1987 edition of the *Complete Notebooks* contains an erroneous transcription of a portion of it. The passage in question is as follows in the 1947 edition:

> what I have gathered from it will perhaps have been exactly some such mastery of fundamental statement—of the art and secret of it, of expression, of the sacred mystery of structure. (p. 208)

In the 1987 edition, however, the following version appears, with the differing words indicated here by italics:

what I have gathered from it will perhaps have been exactly some such *mystery* of fundamental statement—of the art and secret of it, of expression, of the sacred mystery *or* structure. (p. 127)

A check of the original James script, in Houghton Journal IV, shows that the version given in the 1947 edition, and reprinted in my text, is clearly correct.

Chapter 4

1. F. O. Matthiessen, ed., *Stories of Writers and Artists* (New York: New Directions, 1965). Brooke K. Horvath makes note of Matthiessen's exclusion of "The Liar," offering as an explanation that "presumably" it is not, in Matthiessen's words, "primarily about the nature of art or of the artist." And then Horvath proceeds to ignore "The Liar" as well, sticking to the canon established by Matthiessen, without explanation—"presumably" because "The Liar" refuses to conform to the twelve-point structure Horvath offers for our understanding of the writer and artist tales. It would seem that here, as elsewhere, canonicity is determined less by conscious evaluation than by repetitive inertia, deferral to established critical authority, and the selective suppression of texts that will not fit regularized patterns, that persist in making their contradictory claims. See Horvath, "The Life of Art, The Art of Life: The Ascetic Aesthetics of Defeat in James's *Stories of Writers and Artists*," *Modern Fiction Studies* 28.1 (1982): 93–107.

2. Henry James, "The Liar," in Leon Edel, ed., *The Complete Tales of Henry James*, vol. 6 (Philadelphia: Lippincott, 1963), 441. Subsequent references given parenthetically as *LI*.

3. Two studies dealing with "The Liar," those by Barbara Martineau and James Gargano, respectively, have turned away from this question, in favor of more profitable ground elsewhere. Both are perceptive and useful readings, but since they treat only portions of the tale in question, and further restrict the discussions of these portions to their use as instances of a particular Jamesian motif, they are inapposite to the discussion here at hand. See Barbara Martineau, "Portraits are Murdered in the Short Fiction of Henry James," *Journal of Narrative Technique* 2 (1972): 16–25; and James W. Gargano, "The 'Look' as a Major Event in James's Short Fiction," *Arizona Quarterly* 35 (1979): 303–20.

    A more recent and pertinent work is that of Moshe Ron, whose approach and mine resemble each other in several respects. Written contemporaneously, our essays' similarities point up the operative control of a shared critical discourse—even when that very issue is in question—in thus affecting two widely separated writers who happen to choose to deal with the same text. See "The Art of the Portrait According to James," *Yale French Studies* 69 (1985): 222–37.

4. Ray B. West and Robert W. Stallman, eds., *The Art of Modern Fiction* (New York: Rinehart, 1949), 215.

5. Alwyn Berland, *Culture and Conduct in the Novels of Henry James* (Cambridge: Cambridge University Press, 1981), 43.

6. Jones, *James's Psychology*, 197.

7. West and Stallman, *Art of Modern Fiction*, 211.

8. Ibid., 214.

9. Berland, *Culture and Conduct*, 43.

10. Lyall H. Powers, "Henry James and the Ethics of the Artist: 'The Real Thing' and 'The Liar,'" *Texas Studies in Language and Literature* 3 (1961): 365.

11. Marius Bewley, *The Complex Fate* (London: Chatto and Windus, 1952), 86.

12. Powers, "Ethics of the Artist," 360.

13. Ibid., 365.

14. Booth, *Rhetoric of Fiction*, 347.

15. Edward Stone, *The Battle and the Books* (Athens, OH: Ohio University Press, 1964), 83.

16. West and Stallman, *Art of Modern Fiction*, 210.

17. Seltzer, *Henry James and the Art of Power*, 157–58.

18. Foucault, "Discourse on Language," 221.

19. Such a displacement may well illustrate Allon White's point that "the discovery of ambiguities satisfies a hermeneutic desire to proliferate interpretations," a proliferation which, it seems to me, sacrifices self-consistency in order to satisfy an ever-expanding desire. See White, *The Uses of Obscurity*, 131.

20. I have preferred to employ Segal's argument as it originally appeared, as opposed to its recapitulation in book form in *The Lucid Reflector*, because it seems to me that the latter suffers from a certain attenuation as the result of its being reworked to mesh comfortably with the larger context treated there. Cf. Ora Segal, "'The Liar': A Lesson in Devotion," *Review of English Studies* 16 (1965): 272–81; and *The Lucid Reflector* (New Haven: Yale University Press, 1969).

21. Until the projected edition of James's tales as they appeared in serial form is completed, the use of these generally unavailable and unfamiliar versions is simply too impractical. See Maqbool Aziz, ed., *The Tales of Henry James* (Oxford: Clarendon Press, 1973—).

22. James J. Kirschke, *Henry James and Impressionism* (Troy, NY: Whitston, 1981), 237–38.

23. Robert L. Gale, "Names in James," *Names* 14 (1966): 101n.52.

24. Henry James, *The Europeans*, in *The American Novels and Stories of Henry James*, ed. F. O. Matthiessen (New York: Alfred A. Knopf, 1947), 143.

25. Ibid., 118.

26. Henry James, "The Tree of Knowledge," in Leon Edel, ed., *The Complete Tales of Henry James*, vol. 11 (Philadelphia: Lippincott, 1964), 95. Subsequent references given parenthetically as *TK*.

Chapter 5

1. See Alfred R. Ferguson, "Some Bibliographical Notes on the Short Stories of Henry James," *American Literature* 21 (1949): 293.

2. Leon Edel, ed., *The Ghostly Tales of Henry James* (New York: Grosset and Dunlap, 1963), 354–56.

3. See Stone, *The Battle and the Books*.

4. Henry James, "The Third Person," in Leon Edel, ed., *The Complete Tales of Henry James*, vol. 11 (Philadelphia: Lippincott, 1964), 134–35. Subsequent references given parenthetically as *TP*.

5. Shoshana Felman, "Turning the Screw of Interpretation," *Yale French Studies* 55–56 (1977): 164.

6. Cf. Foucault here: "There is no question of there being one category, fixed for all time, reserved for fundamental or creative discourse, and another for those which reiterate, expound and comment. Not a few major texts become blurred and disappear, and commentaries sometimes come to occupy the former position. But while the details of application may well change, the function remains the same, and the principle of hierarchy remains at work. The radical denial of this gradation can never be anything but play, utopia or anguish" ("Discourse on Language," 220). In a sense, what the Misses Frush do at the end of this story is to reassert the boundaries between creative and critical discourses, in a preservation of the hierarchy of voices needed in order to escape the anguish of the ghost.

Chapter 6

1. Adeline Tintner, "Rudyard Kipling and Wolcott Balestier's Literary Collaboration: A Possible Source for James's 'Collaboration,'" *The Henry James Review* 4 (1983): 140–43.

2. Leon Edel, *Henry James: The Middle Years, 1882–1895* (New York: Lippincott, 1962), 319.

3. Ibid., 318.

4. Henry James, "Collaboration," in Leon Edel, ed., *The Complete Tales of Henry James*, vol. 8 (Philadelphia: Lippincott, 1963), 411. Subsequent references given parenthetically as *CO*.

5. Moshe Ron has noted a similarly invested usage of the "studio" elsewhere in James's short fiction, establishing what Ron terms the "rhetorical space of the story." See Moshe Ron, "A Reading of 'The Real Thing,'" *Yale French Studies* 58 (1979): 191.

6. F. O. Matthiessen and Kenneth B. Murdock, eds., *The Notebooks of Henry James* (New York: Oxford University Press, 1947).

Chapter 7

1. See John Carlos Rowe, "James's Rhetoric of the Eye: Re-Marking the Impression," *Criticism* 24 (1982): 233–60; Moshe Ron, "A Reading of 'The Real Thing,'" *Yale French Studies* 58 (1979): 190–212; and Ron, "The Art of the Portrait According to James," *Yale French Studies* 69 (1985): 222–37.

2. The references to these story-ideas in the Notebooks are too numerous and intermingled to allow pinpointing one as especially significant over the others; instead, the reader can look variously at passages found on pp. 130, 169, 179, 192, and 196, among others.

3. It can be argued that there are a number of other James stories taking up exactly this issue, though in differing forms, including "The Real Thing," "The Altar of the Dead," and "The Birthplace"—a list to which I would add "The Liar" and especially "Glasses."

4. Henry James, "The Tone of Time," in Leon Edel, ed., *The Complete Tales of Henry James*, vol. 11 (Philadelphia: Lippincott, 1964), 193. Subsequent references given parenthetically as *TT*.

5. Leon Edel, *Henry James: The Master, 1901–1916* (New York: Lippincott, 1972), 110.

6. Henry James, "Maud-Evelyn," in Leon Edel, ed., *The Complete Tales of Henry James*, vol. 11 (Philadelphia: Lippincott, 1964), 43. Subsequent references given parenthetically as *ME*.

7. Todorov, *The Poetics of Prose*, 145.

8. See Cynthia Ozick, "A Master's Mind," *The New York Times Magazine*, October 26, 1986, 52–55; and Leon Edel, "Introduction: Colloquies with His Good Angel," in Edel and Powers, eds., *The Complete Notebooks of Henry James*.

9. Leon Edel gives a striking account of the burning of the papers in *Henry James: The Master*, pp. 142–43 and 436–37.

10. Lyall H. Powers, "A Note on the Notes," in *The Complete Notebooks of Henry James*, xxiii.

11. Henry James, "Hugh Merrow," in *The Complete Notebooks of Henry James*, 590. Subsequent references given parenthetically as *HM*.

12. Henry James, "The Real Thing," in Leon Edel, ed., *The Complete Tales of Henry James*, vol. 8 (Philadelphia: Lippincott, 1963), 229.

13. Cf. Tzvetan Todorov: "We can see only appearances, and their interpretation remains suspect; only the pursuit of the truth can be present; truth itself, though it provokes the entire movement, remains absent" (*The Poetics of Prose*, 151–52).

14. Edward Said, *Beginnings: Intention and Method* (Baltimore: The Johns Hopkins University Press, 1975), 34.

15. Ibid., 48.

16. Ibid., 71.

Select Bibliography

The following works, whether or not directly cited, formed an indispensable if discordant background noise.

Altieri, Charles. "An Idea and Ideal of a Literary Canon." *Critical Inquiry* 10 (1983): 37–60.

Andreas, Osborn. *Henry James and the Expanding Horizon: A Study of the Meaning and Basic Themes of James's Fiction*. Seattle: University of Washington Press, 1948.

Barthes, Roland. "The Death of the Author." In *Image-Music-Text*. Translated by Stephen Heath. New York: Hill and Wang, 1977.

―――― . *A Lover's Discourse*. Translated by Richard Howard. New York: Hill and Wang, 1978.

Bellman, Samuel Irving. "Henry James's 'The Tree of Knowledge': A Biblical Parallel." *Studies in Short Fiction* 1 (1964): 226–28.

Bercovitch, Sacvan, ed. *Reconstructing American Literary History*. Cambridge: Harvard University Press, 1986.

Berland, Alwyn. *Culture and Conduct in the Novels of Henry James*. Cambridge: Cambridge University Press, 1981.

Bersani, Leo. *A Future for Astyanax: Character and Desire in Literature*. Boston: Little, Brown, 1976.

Bewley, Marius. *The Complex Fate*. London: Chatto and Windus, 1952.

Blackmur, R. P., ed. *The Art of the Novel: Critical Prefaces by Henry James*. New York: Scribner's, 1934.

Bloom, Harold. *The Anxiety of Influence*. New York: Oxford University Press, 1973.

Booth, Wayne. *The Rhetoric of Fiction*. Chicago: University of Chicago Press, 1961.

Bowden, Edwin T. *The Themes of Henry James: A System of Observation through the Visual Arts*. New Haven: Yale University Press, 1956.

Brooke-Rose, Christine. "The Squirm of the True." *PTL* 1 (1976): 265–94, 513–46.

Buitenhuis, Peter. *The Grasping Imagination: The American Writings of Henry James*. Toronto: University of Toronto Press, 1970.

Chambers, Ross. *Story and Situation: Narrative Seduction and the Power of Fiction*. Minneapolis: University of Minnesota Press, 1984.

Chatman, Seymour. *The Later Style of Henry James*. New York: Barnes and Noble, 1972.

Day, Robert Adams. *Told in Letters: Epistolary Fiction before Richardson*. Ann Arbor: University of Michigan Press, 1966.

Dean, Sharon. "The Myopic Narrator in Henry James's 'Glasses.'" *The Henry James Review* 4 (1983): 191–95.

Deleuze, Gilles, and Felix Guattari. *Kafka: Toward a Minor Literature*. Translated by Dana Polan. Minneapolis: University of Minnesota Press, 1986.

Donadio, Stephen. *Nietzsche, Henry James and the Artistic Will*. New York: Oxford University Press, 1978.

Eagleton, Terry. *Literary Theory: An Introduction*. Minneapolis: University of Minnesota Press, 1983.

Edel, Leon. *Henry James: The Untried Years, 1843–1870*. New York: Lippincott, 1953.

————— . *Henry James: The Conquest of London, 1870–1881*. New York: Lippincott, 1962.

————— . *Henry James: The Middle Years, 1882–1895*. New York: Lippincott, 1962.

————— . *Henry James: The Treacherous Years, 1895–1901*. New York: Lippincott, 1969.

————— . *Henry James: The Master, 1901–1916*. New York: Lippincott, 1972.

————— , ed. *The Complete Tales of Henry James*. Philadelphia: Lippincott, 1962–64.

————— , ed. *Henry James: A Collection of Critical Essays*. Englewood Cliffs, NJ: Prentice-Hall, 1963.

Edel, Leon, and Lyall H. Powers, eds. *The Complete Notebooks of Henry James*. New York: Oxford University Press, 1987.

Felman, Shoshana. "Turning the Screw of Interpretation." *Yale French Studies* 55–56 (1977): 94–207.

Ferguson, Alfred R. "Some Bibliographical Notes on the Short Stories of Henry James." *American Literature* 21 (1949): 293–97.

Foucault, Michel. "The Discourse on Language." In *The Archaeology of Knowledge*. Translated by A. M. Sheridan Smith. New York: Random House, 1972.

————— . "What Is an Author?" In *Language, Counter-Memory, Practice: Selected Essays and Interviews*. Edited by Donald F. Bouchard. Translated by Donald F. Bouchard and Sherry Simon. Ithaca: Cornell University Press, 1977.

Gale, Robert L. *The Caught Image: Figurative Language in the Fiction of Henry James*. Chapel Hill: University of North Carolina Press, 1964.

————— . "Names in James." *Names* 14 (1966): 83–108.

Gargano, James W. "The 'Look' as a Major Event in James's Short Fiction." *Arizona Quarterly* 35 (1979): 303–20.

Geismar, Maxwell. *Henry James and His Cult*. London: Chatto and Windus, 1964.

Holland, Laurence B. *The Expense of Vision: Essays on the Craft of Henry James*. Baltimore: Johns Hopkins University Press, 1982.

Horvath, Brooke K. "The Life of Art, the Art of Life: The Ascetic Aesthetics of Defeat in James's *Stories of Writers and Artists*." *Modern Fiction Studies* 28 (1982): 93–107.

Jones, Granville H. *Henry James's Psychology of Experience*. The Hague: Mouton, 1975.

Kappeler, Susanne. *Writing and Reading in Henry James*. London: Macmillan, 1980.

Kelley, Cornelia Pulsifer. *The Early Development of Henry James*, rev. ed. Urbana: University of Illinois Press, 1965.

Kermode, Frank. *The Classic: Literary Images of Permanence and Change*. New York: Viking Press, 1975.

————— . *Forms of Attention*. Chicago: University of Chicago Press, 1985.

————— . "Institutional Control of Interpretation." *Salmagundi* 43 (1979): 72–86.

Kirschke, James J. *Henry James and Impressionism*. Troy, NY: Whitston, 1981.

Kraft, James. *The Early Tales of Henry James*. Carbondale: Southern Illinois University Press, 1969.

Krook, Dorothea. *The Ordeal of Consciousness in Henry James*. Cambridge: Cambridge University Press, 1962.

Margolis, Anne T. *Henry James and the Problem of Audience: An International Act*. Ann Arbor, MI: UMI Research Press, 1985.

Martineau, Barbara. "Portraits are Murdered in the Short Fiction of Henry James." *Journal of Narrative Technique* 2 (1972): 16–25.

Matthiessen, F. O., and Kenneth B. Murdock, eds. *The Notebooks of Henry James*. New York: Oxford University Press, 1947.

McElderry, B. R., Jr. "The Uncollected Stories of Henry James." *American Literature* 21 (1949): 279–91.

Poirier, Richard. *The Comic Sense of Henry James: A Study of the Early Novels.* New York: Oxford University Press, 1960.

Poulet, Georges. *The Metamorphoses of the Circle.* Translated by Carley Dawson and Elliot Coleman. Baltimore: Johns Hopkins University Press, 1966.

Powers, Lyall H. "Henry James and the Ethics of the Artist: 'The Real Thing' and 'The Liar.'" *Texas Studies in Language and Literature* 3 (1961): 360–68.

Renza, Louis A. *"A White Heron" and the Question of Minor Literature.* Madison: University of Wisconsin Press, 1984.

Ron, Moshe. "The Art of the Portrait according to James." *Yale French Studies* 69 (1985): 222–37.

———. "A Reading of 'The Real Thing.'" *Yale French Studies* 58 (1979): 190–212.

Roustang, François. *Dire Mastery: Discipleship from Freud to Lacan.* Translated by Ned Lukacher. Baltimore: Johns Hopkins University Press, 1982.

Rowe, John Carlos. "James's Rhetoric of the Eye: Re-Marking the Impression." *Criticism* 24 (1982): 233–60.

———. *The Theoretical Dimensions of Henry James.* Madison: University of Wisconsin Press, 1984.

Said, Edward. *Beginnings: Intention and Method.* Baltimore: The Johns Hopkins University Press, 1975.

Samuels, Charles Thomas. *The Ambiguity of Henry James.* Urbana: University of Illinois Press, 1971.

Schmitz, Neil. *Of Huck and Alice: Humorous Writing in American Literature.* Minneapolis: University of Minnesota Press, 1983.

Segal, Ora. "'The Liar': A Lesson in Devotion." *Review of English Studies* 16 (1965): 272–81.

———. *The Lucid Reflector.* New Haven: Yale University Press, 1969.

Seltzer, Mark. *Henry James and the Art of Power.* Ithaca: Cornell University Press, 1984.

Smith, Barbara Herrnstein. "Contingencies of Value." *Critical Inquiry* 10 (1983): 1–35.

Stone, Edward. *The Battle and the Books.* Athens, Ohio: Ohio University Press, 1964.

Tanner, Tony. "James's Little Tarts." *The Spectator*, Jan. 4, 1963, p. 19.

Tintner, Adeline. "Poe's 'The Spectacles' and James' 'Glasses.'" *Poe Studies* 9 (1976): 53–54.

———. "Rudyard Kipling and Wolcott Balestier's Literary Collaboration: A Possible Source for James's 'Collaboration.'" *The Henry James Review* 4 (1983): 140–43.

Todorov, Tzvetan. *The Poetics of Prose.* Translated by Richard Howard. Ithaca: Cornell University Press, 1977.

Vaid, Krishna Baldev. *Technique in the Tales of Henry James.* Cambridge: Harvard University Press, 1964.

Von Hallberg, Robert, ed. *Canons.* Chicago: University of Chicago Press, 1984.

West, Ray B., and Robert W. Stallman, eds. *The Art of Modern Fiction.* New York: Rinehart, 1949.

White, Allon. *The Uses of Obscurity: The Fiction of Early Modernism.* London: Routledge and Kegan Paul, 1981.

Index